# FORAGING WASHINGTON

**Help Us Keep This Guide Up to Date**

Every effort has been made by the author and editors to make this guide as accurate and useful as possible. However, many things can change after a guide is published.

We would appreciate hearing from you concerning your experiences with this guide and how you feel it could be improved and kept up to date. While we may not be able to respond to all comments and suggestions, we'll take them to heart, and we'll also make certain to share them with the author. Please send your comments and suggestions to the following email address: editorial@GlobePequot.com.

Thanks for your input, and happy foraging!

# FORAGING WASHINGTON

Finding, Identifying, and Preparing
Edible Wild Foods

Second Edition

## Christopher Nyerges

ESSEX, CONNECTICUT

# FALCONGUIDES®

An imprint of Globe Pequot, the trade division of The Rowman & Littlefield Publishing Group, Inc.
4501 Forbes Blvd., Ste. 200
Lanham, MD 20706
www.rowman.com

Falcon and FalconGuides are registered trademarks and Make Adventure Your Story is a trademark of The Rowman & Littlefield Publishing Group, Inc.

Distributed by NATIONAL BOOK NETWORK

Photos by Christopher Nyerges unless otherwise noted
Maps by Melissa Baker and The Rowman & Littlefield Publishing Group, Inc.

British Library Cataloguing-in-Publication Information available

**Library of Congress Cataloging-in-Publication Data available**

ISBN 978-1-4930-6757-2 (paper: alk. paper)
ISBN 978-1-4930-6758-9 (electronic)

∞™ The paper used in this publication meets the minimum requirements of American National Standard for Information Sciences—Permanence of Paper for Printed Library Materials, ANSI/NISO Z39.48-1992.

Printed in the United States of America

The author and The Rowman & Littlefield Publishing Group, Inc., assume no liability for accidents happening to, or injuries sustained by, readers who engage in the activities described in this book.

The identification, selection, and processing of any wild plant for use as food requires reasonable care and attention to details since, as indicated in the text, certain parts are wholly unsuitable for use and, in some instances, are even toxic. Because attempts to use any wild plants for food depend on various factors controllable only by the reader, the author and Globe Pequot assume no liability for personal accident, illness, or death related to these activities.

*I spent the first forty years of my life woefully unaware of the plant and animal species that share with me the semiarid grassland that is my home. Then I took a "Wild Foods Walk" in the hills where I met Christopher Nyerges, and my education began.*

*I learned about the wild greens, miner's lettuce, purslane, acorns, wild cherries, blackberries, and more—all edible, and quite tasty.*

*After just one class, I felt a great relief that I never experienced as an actor. I realized I was never going to starve.*

*This latest book will make me even more prepared! And you, too, if you're so inclined.*

*A must read!*

*—Ed Begley Jr., actor and environmentalist*

# THE 9 ECOZONES OF WASHINGTON

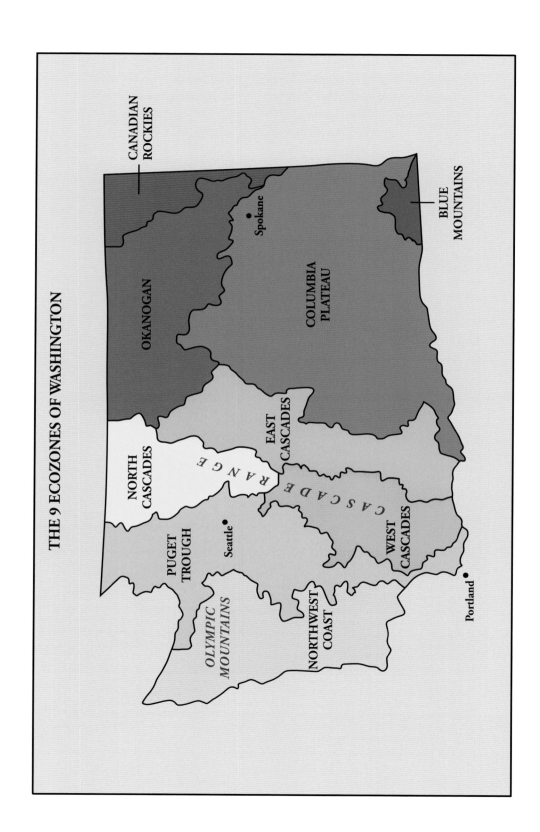

# CONTENTS

# ACKNOWLEDGMENTS

After I had already begun my lifelong study of botany and ethnobotany, I had the very good fortune in approximately 1975 to meet Dr. Leonid Enari. Dr. Enari was the senior biologist at the Los Angeles County Arboretum and taught his course on "Edible, Medicinal, and Poisonous Plants" as well as taxonomy. His knowledge was astronomical.

After I took several of his courses, he allowed me to understudy by coming to his office for private consultations, where he would identify the various plants I brought him and tell me their stories. Never once did I bring him a plant that he didn't know. He eagerly worked with me on my first book (*Guide to Wild Foods*, 1978), assisting me with Latin terms and botanical details. He also worked with me to compile an appendix of safe and primarily edible plant families, which he considered the only legitimate "shortcut" way to study wild foods.

Dr. Enari's unique background in botany and chemistry made him ideally suited as a primary source of information. He earned two higher degrees in both botany and chemistry (the equivalent of a PhD) in his twenties before immigrating to the United States from Estonia, where he experienced some of the results of Nazi occupation. He would tell his students that he pursued these fields because he desired to help people. "With the knowledge of botany and chemistry," he once told our class, "no one need ever go hungry."

When he first moved to the United States, he settled in Portland, Oregon, and taught at Lewis and Clark College and the University of Portland. While living in the Northwest, Dr. Enari researched and wrote *Plants of the Pacific Northwest*, the result of about forty field trips. I have used that book as one of my primary references. He eventually moved to Southern California.

Dr. Enari acted as my teacher, mentor, and friend, and he always encouraged me on to further research as well as teaching and writing. I felt the great loss when he passed away in 2006 at age eighty-nine.

**To Dr. Enari, I Dedicate This Book on Washington Wild Foods.**

I also had many other mentors, teachers, and supporters along the way. These include (but are not limited to) Dr. Luis Wheeler (botanist), Richard Barmakian (nutritionist), Dorothy Poole (Gabrielino "chaparral granny"), Richard E. White (founder of WTI, who taught me how to teach, and how to think), John Watkins (a Mensan who "knew everything"), and Mr. Muir (my botany teacher at John Muir High School). These individuals all imparted some important aspects to me, and they have all been my mentors to varying degrees. I thank them for their influence. Euell Gibbons also had a strong influence on my early studies of wild food, mostly through his books; I met him only once.

Nearly twenty years ago, I met John Kallas, who I regard as the top wild-food man of the Pacific Northwest. Kallas's field trips, workshops, and books are strongly recommended for anyone living in Washington and the surrounding area. With a doctorate in botany, he is a remarkable resource for the Northwest.

Of course there have been many others who taught me bits and pieces along the way, and I am grateful to everyone whose love of the multifaceted art of ethnobotany has touched me in some way. Some of these friends and strong supporters have included Pascal Baudar and Mia Wasilevich, Peter Gail, Gary Gonzales, Dude McLean, Alan Halcon, Paul Campbell, Rick and Karen Adams, Barbara Kolander, Jim Robertson, Timothy Snider, and Dr. Wakeman.

I also want to extend a special thanks to my beloved wife, Helen, for her support of this project!

I also wish to give special thanks to William Schlegel, who assisted with many of the details of this manuscript. I also thank the two other botanists who assisted with this project, who chose to remain unnamed.

## Photo Credits

Yes, I took many of the photographs in this book, but I couldn't do it all by myself. Rick Adams deserves special thanks for the many trips we took together to get the photos. Other folks also contributed photos, including my wife, Helen. I also thank Zoya Akulova, Algie Au, Dan Baird, Jefferey Barrett, Matt Below, Margo Bors, Barry Breckling, Kyle Chamberlain, Tom Elpel, Roger George, H. Tim Gladwin, Gary Gonzales, William J. Hartman, Barbara Kolander, Bob Krumm, Louis-M. Landry, Jeff Martin, Steve Matson, Keir Morse, Julie Kierstead Nelson, Jean Pawek, Jim Robertson, Vickie Shufer, Bob Sivinski, Vernon Smith, Robert Steers, Simon Tonge, Dr. Amadej Trnkoczy, Lily Jane Tsong, and Mary Winter.

# INTRODUCTION

We owe a debt of gratitude to the generations of indigenous peoples of North America whose life and livelihood depended on plants for food and everything else. Much of this knowledge has been passed down generation to generation, and much has been rediscovered by researchers.

Many of the living "old ways" have been lost, but the knowledge of how to utilize the plants of the land has not been entirely forgotten. Various generations have realized the great value of knowing how to identify and use what nature has provided, even though this information waxes and wanes in importance in the general viewpoint.

When there is war or depression or famine, we desire to rekindle this link to our past, and hope for our future. When times are good, and money flows, we forget our roots. Just fifty years ago, you were considered poor, to be pitied, if you actually used wild foods.

With Euell Gibbons in the early 1970s, the tide began to turn again, and today everyone wants to know at least a little about our national heritage of wild foods. Everyone wants to be self-sufficient and be a part of the solution. And today we have an abundance of books, videos, and classes to teach us these skills.

In addition to the native flora, we now have an abundance of introduced plants and common edible weeds, which were used for generations throughout Europe and Asia. Sometimes these introduced flora are a blessing, sometimes not.

## Scope of This Book

*Foraging Washington* intends to cover plants that can be used primarily for food and are common in Washington. We are not attempting to cover every single edible plant that could possibly be used for food, or those that are very marginal as food. Our focus is on those wild foods that are widespread, easily recognizable and identifiable, and are sufficient to create meals. Many of the wild edibles that are too localized, or only provide a marginal source of food, are not included. Plants that are endangered or have the possibility of being endangered have not been included. In general, plants that are too easily confused with something poisonous have also been omitted. Mushrooms are not included.

The content of this book is intended to be useful for hikers and backpackers and for anyone in urban areas where so many of these plants still grow. Our goal is to provide a book that details the plants that a person attempting to live off the land would actually be eating.

If you embark on the study of ethnobotany, and start working closely with a mentor/teacher, your learning will expand way beyond the pages of this book, and that is how it should be.

This is not a book about medicinal properties, and though some medicinal aspects will be addressed in passing, we will provide some ideal references in the back of the book. Nor does this book focus on native plants exclusively. If you're hungry in the woods, or in your own backyard, you don't care if the plant is native or introduced, right?

## Organization

The plants in this book are organized according to the system used by botanists.

Many books on plants organize the plants by flower color or environmental niche, both of which have their adherents and their pitfalls. However, this book categorizes the plants according to their families, which gives you a broader perspective on many more plants than can be reasonably put into one book. As you will see, many of the genera (and some families) are entirely safe to use as food. This is how I was taught by my teacher and mentor, Dr. Leonid Enari, since he believed that—though there is no shortcut to learning about the identity and uses of plants—understanding the families will impart a far greater insight into the scope of "wild foods."

We'll start with the "lower" plants, then the gymnosperms (the cone-bearing plants), and then the flowering plants, in alphabetical order by their Latin family names.

# PLANTS LISTED BY ENVIRONMENT TYPE

In our selection of plants for *Foraging Washington*, we've attempted to include common edible plants from the different environments of the state.

Washington has a tremendous diversity of ecosystems: marine waters, tide pools, estuaries, rain forests, dry coniferous forests, subalpine and alpine meadows and parklands, shrub-steppe, grasslands, prairies, sand dunes, riparian areas, and a variety of freshwater wetland types.

Just look at a map of the state, from the riches of the Northwest coast region, to Puget Sound, the Cascade range running from north to south more or less through the middle of the state, with the unique ecosystems of foothill, mountain, and alpine, to the semidesert Columbia Plateau. These unique environments provided the food and riches for the estimated 125 distinct Northwest tribes (speaking 50 languages) who lived here before the arrival of the Euro-Americans. It is believed that human occupation occurred here nearly 10,000 years ago. The people subsisted on hunting, fishing, and the abundant wild plants.

Though there are different systems of classifying the environments of Washington, here are nine ecoregions that describe the entire state.

## THE NINE ECOREGIONS OF WASHINGTON

### NORTHWEST COAST ECOREGION
*This ecoregion includes plants found in the following environments*: Coast, Coast Forest, Riparian, Subalpine Forest, Alpine, Mountain Forest, and Urban/Developed.

The Pacific Northwest Coast ecoregion includes most of the Olympic Peninsula of Washington.

Washington's westernmost and wettest ecoregion extends from ocean depths to the Olympic Mountains' glaciated peaks.

The Northwest Coast ecoregion fronts roughly 150 miles of ocean shoreline and encompasses roughly 11 percent of Washington State, from the Canadian border to the mouth of the Columbia River.

The western edge of the Northwest Coast is an example of a temperate rain forest, with more than a dozen feet of rainfall a year on average—and mild temperatures.

In the alpine heights of the Olympic Mountains, wildflowers grow abundantly through their short season. Here there are marshes, fens, ponds, and seasonal wet meadows, along with riparian and herbaceous wetlands, each hosting its own suite of plants and animals.

## PUGET TROUGH ECOREGION

*This ecoregion includes plants found in the following environments*: Coast, Coast Forest, Interior Forest/Cedar Hemlock, Bunchgrass/Steppe, and Urban/Developed.

The Puget Trough ecoregion includes Puget Sound and surrounding foothills.

A great inland arm of the sea—Puget Sound—is flanked by forested foothills and freshened by many rivers. The Puget Trough ecoregion is home to over 75 percent of Washington's population.

Many of the planet's most impressive stands of trees grow here, along with a mix of riparian habitats, oak woodlands, and prairies.

The vegetation in most of the ecoregion's landscapes has now been altered due to the development of cities and managed forests; agricultural lands changed the vegetation, and the landscapes face pressure from sprawling development.

Here in the understory we find ferns, Oregon grape, salmonberry, and many others. Other key trees are Pacific madrone, a frequent feature on dry bluffs, and Oregon ash, common in riparian areas—south toward the Columbia River.

Washington has one native species of oak, the Garry oak. It is often associated with grasslands. These grasslands are one of the most threatened ecosystems in Washington. They support spectacular floral displays, including blue camas.

## NORTH CASCADES ECOREGION

*This ecoregion includes plants found in the following environments*: Interior Forest/Cedar Hemlock, Mountain Forest, Subalpine Forest, Alpine, Bunchgrass/Steppe, and Riparian.

The North Cascades ecoregion contains some of the largest expanses of wilderness in the lower forty-eight states. This ecoregion (about 10 percent of Washington) includes the Cascade Mountains north of Snoqualmie Pass and west of the Cascade crest northward into British Columbia.

The vegetation here is highly diverse. At lower elevations, forests of Douglas-fir, western red cedar, and western hemlock intermix with riparian areas that support broadleaf trees such as red alder and big-leaf maple.

## WEST CASCADES ECOREGION

*This ecoregion includes plants found in the following environments:* Alpine, Subalpine Forest, Cedar Hemlock, and Riparian.

The West Cascades ecoregion encompasses the west-side midsection of the great Cascades cordillera. In Washington, the West Cascades run southward from Snoqualmie Pass to the Columbia Gorge, the only lowland divide in the range. Across the Columbia, the West Cascades ecoregion extends south into Oregon.

The crest of the Cascades marks the ecoregion's eastern edge. The western boundary dips to meet the foothills of the Puget Trough at about 1,000 feet. This sparsely populated ecoregion covers about 8 percent of Washington's population.

The wet and relatively mild conditions in the West Cascades support magnificent conifer forests. In lowland areas of Mount Rainier National Park, patches of old-growth rain forest still support trees up to 1,000 years old. These ancient Douglas-firs offer habitat for dozens of additional plant and fungal species.

Up to elevations of roughly 11,000 feet, the volcanoes in the West Cascades host alpine meadows and heath fields.

## EAST CASCADES ECOREGION
*This ecoregion includes plants found in the following environments*: Subalpine Forest, Mountain Forest, Ponderosa Pine, Sagebrush, Bunchgrass/Steppe, Riparian, and Urban/Developed.

The East Cascades ecoregion includes the mountains that lie east of the Cascade crest and the foothills as they flatten into the Columbia Plateau. In Washington, it stretches from roughly Lake Chelan in the north to the Columbia River Gorge in the south.

On the dry side of the Cascades lies one of Washington's most diverse ecoregions, rich in biological wealth from its montane crest down through open stands of ponderosa pine and Garry oak to the edge of the sagebrush steppe.

The East Cascade ecoregion is one of Washington's most heavily forested areas.

At the crest, subalpine fir, whitebark pine, Engelmann spruce, and mountain hemlock prevail. At mid-elevations, roughly 4,000 to 6,000 feet, forests shift to a mix of western larch and lodgepole pine. Lower yet, ponderosa pine and Douglas-fir forest, with an understory of snowberry and Idaho fescue, is widespread and characteristic.

In the south of the ecoregion, Garry oak woodlands are common in the foothills. The lowest elevations of the East Cascades ecoregion dry out considerably.

The ponderosa pine and Douglas-fir forests yield to big sagebrush and bunch-grass, the shrub-steppe vegetation of the Columbia Plateau.

## OKANOGAN ECOREGION
*This ecoregion includes plants found in the following environments*: Alpine, Subal-pine Forest, Mountain Forest, Sagebrush, Bunchgrass/Steppe, Ponderosa Pine, Riparian, and Urban/Developed/Farmland.

The Okanogan ecoregion could be called the mountains between mountains—the broad highland area separating the North Cascades and the Northern Rock-ies in northeastern Washington.

In north-central Washington, the Cascades, the Rockies, and the Columbia Plateau converge to form the Okanogan ecoregion, which boasts highland landscapes and lowland waterways.

In Washington, the ecoregion covers about 14 percent of the state. It extends significantly into the sage-steppe country of south-central British Columbia.

In the Okanogan ecoregion, native plant cover ranges from alpine tundra to semiarid shrub. The ecoregion's plant communities vary with elevation.

## CANADIAN ROCKY MOUNTAINS ECOREGION
*This ecoregion includes plants found in the following environments*: Alpine, Moun-tain Forest, Riparian, Bunchgrass/Steppe, Ponderosa Pine, and Subalpine Forest.

Some of Washington's wildest country is found in its far northeastern corner.

The western edge of the Rocky Mountains forms this ecoregion in Washing-ton's northeastern corner. Composed primarily of the Selkirk Mountains, it encompasses 4 percent of the state.

In Washington, the ecoregion is bounded by the Okanogan ecoregion on the west and touches the Columbia Plateau ecoregion on its southwestern edge. The ecoregion is sparsely populated.

The Canadian Rocky Mountains ecoregion supports Rocky Mountain plants at the edge of their range in Washington. Alpine meadows, dense coniferous forests, riparian woodlands, and rolling grasslands are all found here.

Along rivers, streams, and lakes, herbaceous wetlands are common. Grass-lands can be found on the lower foothills and on higher hillsides with south-ern exposures.

## BLUE MOUNTAINS ECOREGION

*This ecoregion includes plants found in the following environments:* Bunchgrass/Steppe, Subalpine Forest, Sagebrush, and Riparian.

The Blue Mountains spill over into Washington's extreme southeastern corner. They are the westernmost ranges of the Middle Rockies that extend south into Oregon and east across central Idaho and into Montana.

Washington's smallest ecoregion, the rugged Blue Mountains are a rolling high plateau dotted with ponderosa pine forests, vestiges of Palouse Prairie, and steeply cut rimrock canyons.

Vegetation changes dramatically as hillsides plunge toward river bottoms along the Grande Ronde and Snake. In the higher canyons, shrublands can be found. Western juniper, snowberry, mountain mahogany, bitterbrush, and sage are among the shrubs found in the Blue Mountains.

At lower elevations, grasslands are common. Patches of shrub-steppe are found here, though much of the grasslands and shrub-steppe have been displaced by agricultural operations.

## COLUMBIA PLATEAU ECOREGION

*This ecoregion includes plants found in the following environments:* Bunchgrass/Steppe, Sagebrush, Riparian, and Urban/Developed/Farm.

The semiarid Columbia Plateau occupies nearly one-third of the state. It is bordered by the Cascades to the west, the Okanogan Highlands to the north, the Rockies to the east, and the Blue Mountains to the southeast.

Two great rivers, the Columbia and the Snake, dominate the dramatic dry landscape of Washington's largest ecoregion—home to an inland sea of sagebrush and the state's fertile agricultural heartland.

The Columbia Plateau is dominated by shrub-steppe, like much of the Great Basin. This is a once-expansive habitat of shrubs, forbs, and bunchgrass. Aromatic shrubs such as sagebrush and bitterbrush offer good browsing to a wide range of wildlife. Other plant communities can be found in this semiarid region, including salt desert scrub and native grasslands. Herbaceous wetlands, such as potholes, marshes, and wet meadows, are found throughout the Columbia Plateau. Their aquatic plants, rushes, and thickets of shrubs constitute another conservation priority.

## TYPES OF ENVIRONMENTS IN WASHINGTON

The following lists show only the plants discussed in this book and the environments in which they are most likely to be found. Some plants are found in more than one environment.

### COAST

Beach strawberry (*Fragaria chiloensis*)
Cattail (*Typha* spp.)
Crabapple
Fennel (*Foeniculum vulgare*)
Glasswort (*Salicornia* spp.)
Rush (*Juncus textilis* and others)
Sea rocket (*Cakile edentula* and *C. maritima*)
Seaweeds (Chlorophyta, Phaeophyta, Rhodophyta)
Violet (*Viola* spp.)

### COAST FOREST

Blackberry
Blueberry (*Vaccinium corymbosum, V. uliginosum*)
Bracken
Camas
Cherries
Crabapple
Elderberry (red)
Hazelnut
Huckleberry (evergreen and red)
Indian plum
Kinnikinnick
Madrone
Miner's lettuce (*Claytonia sibirica*)
Oregon grape (*Mahonia nervosa*)
Oregon oak
Rose
*Rubus* spp.
Salal
Salmonberry
Serviceberry/Saskatoon
Sheep sorrel
Sour grass
Spring beauty
Strawberry
Trailing blackberry
Violet
Wild crabapple (*Malus fusca*)

### RIPARIAN

American bistort (*Bistorta bistortoides*)
Bracken (*Pteridium aquilinum*)
Brook saxifrage
Burdock
Cattail
Cow Parsnip (*Heracleum maximum,* formerly *H. lanatum*)
Grasses (*Glyceria grandis* and *Phalaris arundinacea*)
Hazelnut
Mint (*Mentha* spp.)
Monkey flower (*Mimulus guttatus*)
Nettle (*Urtica dioica*)
Rush (*Juncus textilis* and others)
Serviceberry
Veronica (*Veronica americana*)
Violet
Wapato
Watercress (*Nasturtium officinale*)

## SUBALPINE FOREST

Avalanche lily
Bracken
Brook saxifrage
Camas (in meadows)
Cow parsnip
Currant
Elderberry
Fireweed
Huckleberry (*Vaccinium membranaceum*)
Kinnikinnick
Mountain bluebells (*Mertensia ciliata*)
Mountain sorrel (*Oxyria digyna*)
Pine
Raspberry
Serviceberry
Spring beauty
Stinging nettle
Strawberry
Thimbleberry
Thistle
Wild onion

## ALPINE TUNDRA/ALPINE

Avalanche lily
American bistort
Fireweed
Huckleberry
Mountain bluebells
Mountain sorrel

## MOUNTAIN FOREST/PONDEROSA PINE/INTERIOR FOREST/ CEDAR-HEMLOCK

Arrowleaf balsamroot
Biscuit root
Bracken
Chokecherry
Crabapple
Currant
Elderberry (blue)
Fireweed
Glacier lily
Hazelnut
Highbush cranberry
Huckleberry
Kinnikinnick
Miner's lettuce
Oregon grape
Oregon oak (*Quercus garryana*) (central Washington)
Pine
Prickly lettuce
Raspberry
*Rubus* spp.
Salsify
Serviceberry/Saskatoon
Spring beauty
Strawberry
Thimbleberry
Thistle
Violet
Wild onion
Wild rose
Yampa

## BUNCHGRASS/STEPPE/SAGEBRUSH

Arrowleaf balsamroot
Biscuit root
Blueberry
Camas
Chokecherry
Elder
Golden currant
Mustard
Oregon grape

Oregon oak
Prickly lettuce
Salsify
Serviceberry/Saskatoon
Thistle
Wild asparagus
Wild onion
Yampa

## URBAN/DEVELOPED

Amaranth
Apple: crabapple and feral domestic
  apple
Bittercress
Blackberry
Black nightshade
Burdock
Cat's ear
Chickweed
Chicory
Crabapple
Curly dock
Dandelion
Fennel
Lamb's quarter
Mallow
Mint
Mustard
Nipplewort
Oregon grape

Oregon oak
Pine
Pineapple weed
Plantain
Prickly lettuce
*Prunus* spp.
Purslane
Salsify
Sheep sorrel
Shepherd's purse
Sour grass
Sow thistle
Stinging nettle
Thistle
Violet
Wild asparagus
Wild carrot
Wild radish
Wild rose
Wintercress

# COLLECTING AND HARVESTING WILD FOODS

As more and more of us are desiring to learn how to "live off the land" and using wild plants for food and medicine, it is necessary to practice sustainable collecting and harvesting methods.

The art (and science) of foraging is a sacred art, passed down from generation to generation, from the beginning of time. It is a fundamental skill, letting the fruits of the land feed you, as you in turn do everything you can to maintain the health and integrity of the land. People of the past instinctively knew that their survival was intimately tied to the health of the land. You could not overharvest, overgraze, and exploit without severe consequences. Remember: We and the land are one. It is an unfortunate point of modern days that this simple fact is being forgotten.

Always make sure it is both legal and safe for you to harvest the wild foods. Legality can usually be determined simply by asking a few questions or making a phone call. In some cases, when we're dealing with public lands, the issue of legality may be a bit more difficult to ascertain.

You also want to be safe, making sure there are no agricultural or commercial toxins near and around the plants you intend to harvest. Again, it pays in the long run to carefully observe the surroundings and to ask a few questions.

Foraging has gotten more popular in the last few years for some very good reasons. People want to reconnect with their roots, and discover how our ancestors lived off the land. We're also discovering that wild foods not only taste good, but they are also generally far more nutritious than just about everything from the modern supermarket.

So when you forage, be sure to set a good example both in how you forage and in what you forage. Don't uproot plants if you don't need to. Don't overharvest any area. And keep in mind that much of the landscape is overrun with invasive non-native plants, the so-called "weeds," mostly from Europe. There is usually a nearly unlimited amount of these plants, and you are usually welcome to collect them.

There has been some backlash recently by those who feel foragers are ruining the landscape. I would agree that in some very narrow instances, this has been the case—typically with mushroom collectors and collectors of herbs for "smudge bundles." I implore you to develop a relationship with the plants, and learn how to harvest safely and sustainably. It is not that hard to be a conscientious forager, and in some cases, you might actually see an increase in the number, size, and health of wild plants by your very careful thinning, pruning, and collecting. If you consider how the human race moved from forager to farmer, it was precisely through this careful and intimate relationship with the plants—benefiting both parties—that early farming methods developed.

It is unfortunate that modern farming—far more than foraging—negatively affects vast swaths of native vegetation all over the globe, something we regard as a necessary aspect of food production. (*That's another story, of course. However, I strongly encourage you to learn more about how food is produced these days. Some good references in this regard are* Everything I Want to Do Is Illegal *by Joel Salatin and* In Defense of Food *by Michael Pollan. Both books give you a good picture of modern food production, the many problems therein, and some practical solutions—one of which is to eat wild foods!*)

Unless it is the root that you are using for food, you should never need to uproot a plant, especially if it is only the leaves that you intend to eat.

I have documented in my *Extreme Simplicity* book how I was able to extend the life of many annual weeds by carefully pinching back the leaves that I wanted to eat, and then allowing the plant to grow back before picking again. Even when I believe that someone else will pull up the plant later or plow the area, I still do not uproot the plants on general principle. If I leave the plant rooted, the root system is good for the soil and the plant continues to manufacture oxygen. Various insects and birds might eat the bugs on the plant or its seeds. Let life continue.

When you are harvesting greens, snippers can be used, but usually nothing is needed but your fingernails and maybe a sharp knife. Cut what you need, don't deplete an area, and move on.

Harvesting seeds is done when the plant is at the end of its annual cycle, but there is still no reason to uproot the plant. When I harvest curly dock or lamb's quarter seed, I carefully try to get as much into my bag as possible. I know that some seed is being scattered, and that's a good thing for next season. I also know that a few seeds are still on the stalk, and that's a good thing for the birds in the area.

I nearly always harvest in an area of abundance. If there are very few specimens there, my usual course of action is to simply leave them alone.

You will note when you read this book that I advise foragers to leave the wild onions in the ground and to eat the greens. However, in cases of abundance, your thinning the roots will help stimulate more growth, and that is a good thing, akin to the passive agricultural practices of the Native Americans who once exclusively lived here.

In general, foraging doesn't require many tools. You will need bags—plastic, cloth, paper—whatever is appropriate for the food item. In some cases, you harvest with buckets or tubs. Usually no other tools are needed, though I generally carry a Florian ratchet clipper for any cutting, as well as a knife or two. I rarely need a trowel, though it comes in handy with some harvesting.

The more you forage, the more you'll realize that your best tool is your memory. You'll learn to recognize where the mushrooms grow, where the berry vines are, and the fields that will be full of chickweed next spring. And the more you know, the less you'll need to carry.

# HOW MUCH WILD FOOD IS OUT THERE, ANYWAY?

**Plants Everywhere, but Not All Can Be Eaten**

In his insightful book *Participating in Nature*, Thomas Elpel has created a unique chart, based on his years of observation and analysis, to give a perspective on the sheer numbers of edible, medicinal, and poisonous plants. Elpel is also the author of *Botany in a Day*.

First, almost every plant with known ethnobotanical uses can be used medicinally; even some otherwise toxic plants can be used medicinally if you know the right doses and proper application. So, yes, medicine is everywhere. But nearly two-thirds of these plants are neither poisonous nor used for food for various reasons.

The extremely poisonous plants that will outright kill you are rare. And since there are so few of these deadly plants, it is not all that difficult to learn to identify them. In Washington, for example, there is poison hemlock, death camas, and a few others, which can be easily confused for something edible. Others that could cause death are various mushrooms and certain commonly planted ornamentals, such as oleander. It is not uncommon to hear about mushroom sickness and even death.

Though only a few plants are deadly poisonous, many more would make you very sick but not normally kill you. Still, all the poisonous and toxic plants combined are just a very small percentage of all the known ethnobotanicals.

Edible plants compose maybe a quarter of the known edible, medicinal, and poisonous plants. Of the plants that we normally think of as "food plants," the overwhelming majority provide us primarily with greens. That is, throughout most of the year, the majority of the food that you'll obtain from the wild consists of greens: food to make salads and stir-fries and add to soups and vegetable dishes. These are plants that will not by themselves create a filling and balanced meal, but they will add vitamins and minerals to your dried beans, MREs (meals ready to eat), freeze-dried camping food, and other foods. In general, greens are not high sources of protein, fats, or carbohydrates.

Berries and fruits compose another category of wild foods. Maybe 10 percent of the wild foods you find will consist of berries or fruits, but timing is everything. Unlike greens, which you can usually find year-round, fruits and berries are typically available only seasonally, so if you want some during other times of the year, you'll need to dry them or make jams or preserves. This includes blackberries, elderberries, mulberries, and many others. They provide sugar and flavor, but, like greens, you would not make a meal entirely from fruits and berries.

An even smaller category of wild foods, perhaps about 5 percent, consists of starchy roots, such as cattails and Jerusalem artichokes. These are great for energy, though they may not be available year-round. This is why these foods have traditionally been dried, even powdered, and stored for use later in the year.

Another small category of wild foods consists of the seeds and nuts. This includes grass seeds, pine nuts, and acorns, among many others. It is in this small category, probably less than 5 percent of wild foods, where you obtain the carbohydrates, oils, and sometimes proteins that constitute the "staff of life." Though these are not available year-round, some have a longer harvest time than others. Some may have a harvest period of as short as two weeks. Many grass seeds simply fall to the ground and are eaten by animals. Fortunately, most of these can be harvested in season and stored for later use.

# ARE WILD FOODS NUTRITIOUS?

It is a common misconception that "wild foods" are neither nutritious nor tasty. Both of these points are erroneous, as anyone who has actually taken the time to identify and use wild foods can testify. I've had many new students who had been convinced of the nutritional value of wild foods, but had assumed that the plants nevertheless tasted bad. Of course, a bad cook can make even the best foods unpalatable. And if you pick wild foods and don't clean them, don't use just the tender sections, and don't prepare them properly, you'll almost certainly turn people off to wild foods.

Wild foods are not only nutritious but can also be as flavorful as any food in the finest restaurants.

For your edification, here is a chart extracted from the USDA's *Composition of Foods* to give you an idea of the nutritional content of common wild foods.

## Nutritional Composition of Wild Foods (per 100 grams, unless otherwise indicated)

Blanks denote no data available; dashes denote lack of data for a constituent believed to be present in measurable amounts. Only a select number of plants for which we had data are represented.

| Plant | Calories | Protein (g) | Fat (g) | Calcium (mg) | Phosphorus (mg) | Iron (mg) | Sodium (mg) | Potassium (mg) | Vitamin A (IU) | Thiamine (mg) | Riboflavin (mg) | Niacin (mg) | Vitamin C (mg) | Part |
|---|---|---|---|---|---|---|---|---|---|---|---|---|---|---|
| Amaranth | 36 | 3.5 | 0.5 | 267 | 67 | 3.9 | – | 411 | 6,100 | 0.08 | 0.16 | 1.4 | 80 | Leaf, raw |
| Carob | | 4.5 | | 352 | 81 | 2.9 | 35 | 827 | 14 | | 0.4 | 1.89 | 0.2 | Pods |
| Cattail | | 8% | 2% | | | | | | | | | | | Rhizomes |
| Chia seed | | 20.2% | | 631 | 860 | 7.72 | 16 | 407 | 54 | 0.62 | 0.17 | 8.8 | 1.6 | Seed |
| CHICORY TRIBE | | | | | | | | | | | | | | |
| • Chicory | 20 | 1.8 | 0.3 | 86 | 40 | 0.9 | – | 420 | 4,000 | 0.06 | 0.1 | 0.5 | 22 | Leaf, raw |
| • Dandelion | 45 | 2.7 | 0.7 | 187 | 66 | 3.1 | 76 | 397 | 14,000 | 0.19 | 0.26 | – | 35 | Leaf, raw |
| • Sow thistle | 20 | 2.4 | 0.3 | 93 | 35 | 3.1 | – | – | 2,185 | 0.7 | 0.12 | 0.4 | 5 | Leaf, raw |
| Chickweed | | | | | | | | | | | | | | |
| Dock | 28 | 2.1 | 0.3 | 66 | 41 | 1.6 | 5 | 338 | 12,900 | 0.09 | 0.22 | 0.5 | 119 | Leaf, raw |
| Fennel | 28 | 2.8 | 0.4 | 100 | 51 | 2.7 | – | 397 | 3,500 | – | – | – | 31 | Leaf, raw |
| Grass | | | | | | | | | | 300 to 500 IU | 2,000 to 2,800 IU | – | 300 to 700 mg | Leaf, raw |
| Jerusalem artichoke | 75 | 2.3 | 0.1 | 14 | 78 | 3.4 | – | – | 20 | 0.2 | 0.06 | 1.3 | 4 | Root, raw |
| Lamb's quarter | 43 | 4.2 | 0.8 | 309 | 72 | 1.2 | 43 | 452 | 11,600 | 0.16 | 0.44 | 1.2 | 80 | Leaf, raw |
| Mallow | 37 | 4.4 | 0.6 | 249 | 69 | 12.7 | – | – | 2,190 | 0.13 | 0.2 | 1.0 | 35 | Leaf |
| Milkweed | – | 0.8 | 0.5 | – | – | – | – | – | – | – | – | – | – | Leaf |
| Miner's lettuce | | | | | | 10% RDA | | | 22% RDA | | | | 33% RDA | Leaf |
| MUSTARD FAMILY | | | | | | | | | | | | | | |
| • Mustard | 31 | 3 | 0.5 | 183 | 50 | 3 | 32 | 377 | 7,000 | 0.12 | 0.22 | 0.8 | 97 | Leaf |

| | | | | | | | | | | | | | | |
|---|---|---|---|---|---|---|---|---|---|---|---|---|---|---|
| • Shepherd's purse | 33 | 4.2 | 0.5 | 208 | 86 | 4.8 | – | 394 | 1,554 | 0.08 | 0.17 | 0.4 | 36 | Leaf |
| • Watercress | 19 | 2.2 | 0.3 | 120 | 60 | 0.2 | 41 | 330 | 3,191 | | 0.12 | 0.2 | 43 | Leaf |
| Nettle | 65 | 5.5 | 0.7 | 481 | 71 | 1.64 | 4 | 334 | 2,011 | – | 0.16 | 0.38 | 76 | Leaf |
| New Zealand spinach | 19 | 2.2 | 0.3 | 58 | 46 | 2.6 | 159 | 795 | 4,300 | 0.04 | 0.17 | 0.6 | 30 | Leaf, raw |
| Oak (acorn flour) | 65% carbo-hydrates | 6% | 18% | 43 | 103 | 1.21 | 0 | 712 | 51 | 0.1 | 0.1 | 2.3 | 0 | Nut |
| ONION FAMILY | | | | | | | | | | | | | | |
| • Chives | 28 | 1.8 | 0.3 | 69 | 44 | 1.7 | – | 250 | 5,800 | 0.08 | 0.13 | 0.5 | 56 | Leaf, raw |
| • Garlic | 137 | 6.2 | 0.2 | 29 | 202 | 1.5 | 19 | 529 | – | 0.25 | 0.08 | 0.5 | 15 | Clove, raw |
| • Onion | 36 | 1.5 | 0.2 | 51 | 39 | 1 | 5 | 231 | 2,000 | 0.05 | 0.05 | 0.4 | 32 | Young leaf, raw |
| Passion fruit [per pound] | | | | 31 | 151 | 3.8 | 66 | 831 | 1,650 | | | | 71 | Fruit |
| Pine nuts | 635 | 12 | 60.5 | | 604 | 5.2 | – | | | 1.28 | | | | Nut |
| Prickly pear | 42 | 0.5 | 0.1 | 20 | 28 | 0.3 | 2 | 166 | 60 | 0.01 | 0.03 | 0.4 | 22 | Fruit, raw |
| Purslane | 21 | 30 | 1.7 | 0.4 | 103 | 39 | 3.5 | – | – | 2,500 | 0.03 | 0.1 | 0.5 | Leaf and stem, raw |
| Rose | 162 | 1.6 | | 169 | 61 | 1.06 | 4 | 429 | 4,345 | | 0.16 | 1.3 | 426 | Fruit, raw |
| SEAWEED | | | | | | | | | | | | | | |
| • Dulse | – | – | 3.2 | 296 | 267 | – | 2,085 | 8,060 | – | – | – | – | – | "Leaf" |
| • Irish moss | – | – | 1.8 | 885 | 157 | 8.9 | 2,892 | 2,844 | – | – | – | – | – | "Leaf" |
| • Kelp | – | – | 1.1 | 1,093 | 240 | – | 3,007 | 5,273 | – | – | – | – | – | "Leaf" |

Primary source: *Composition of Foods*, US Department of Agriculture

# Seaweeds

Bull kelp JAY HARTMAN OF SEATTLE

# MARINE GREEN ALGAE (Chlorophyta)

About 5,000 species, including sea lettuce, etc. In Washington, this group is represented by sea lettuce (*Ulva lactuca*) and others.

# BROWN ALGAE (Phaeophyta)

Approximately 1,000 species, including all kelps, rockweed, etc. In Washington, this group is represented by alaria (*Alaria marginata*), bull whip kelp (*Nereocystis luetkeana*), and fucus, among others.

# RED ALGAE (Rhodophyta)

The most abundant seaweed of the world, with over 4,000 species, including Irish moss, dulse, laver, etc. In Washington, this group is represented by nori (*Porphyra* spp.), Turkish towel (*Chondracanthus* spp.), and others.

**Use:** Food (depending on the species, some are eaten dried, cooked, raw, or pickled); nutrition; utility

**Range:** Ocean and beaches

**Similarity to toxic species:** See "Cautions."

**Best time:** Available year-round

**Status:** Relatively common

**Tools needed:** Bucket, gloves

## PROPERTIES

You don't need to be a botanist to recognize seaweeds. Most people know them when they see them—floating in the surf or lying on the sand. They grow in a wide array of colors, sizes, and shapes. The kelps are perhaps the most conspicuous along the coast, with their long stipes and characteristic fronds. They often lie in masses on the beach.

In general, seaweeds have leaflike fronds, stipes that resemble the stems of terrestrial plants, and holdfasts that resemble roots. Some seaweeds are very delicate; others are very tough and almost leathery. Many have hollow sections—"floats"—which allow them to float more readily.

Others are like thin sheets of wet plastic, such as sea lettuce. Their colors generally indicate their category of green, brown, or red marine algae.

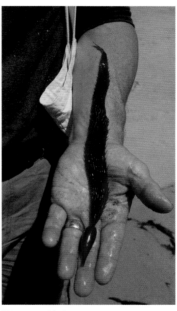

Close-up of kelp RICK ADAMS

## USES

Seaweeds are not only tasty (when prepared properly) but also very nutritious.

When I was originally researching seaweeds, I spoke with botanists, marine biologists, and even a seaweed specialist. Some believed that all seaweeds—all the thousands of varieties—are a completely nontoxic group of plants, and most agreed that these are all safe to consume. The more conservative viewpoint had to do with the fact that there are so *many* seaweeds, and that not all have been studied enough to make such a blanket statement. Nevertheless, seaweeds are collectively regarded as highly nutritious and generally edible. One hundred grams of kelp, for example, contains 1,093 mg of calcium, 240 mg of phosphorus, and 5,273 mg of potassium! And these iodine-rich foods can be used in a variety of ways.

**Kelp holdfast** RICK ADAMS

Some—such as sea lettuce, which actually looks like lettuce—can be washed and added raw to salads. Others are best dried and then used as a seasoning to other foods. Some seaweeds can be diced and added to soups and stews. And most can be simply dried and powdered and then used as a salt substitute or flavor enhancer.

Raw, dried, powdered, or cooked, seaweeds represent the closest thing to a "fast food" that you'll find from the wild.

If you live near the coast and have easy access to seaweeds, I encourage you to research the many specific seaweeds that are used for food, and—via the myriad books exclusively about seaweeds—learn the various ways to prepare them. And experiment! Unless you are lost and haven't the time to experiment or research, there are many sources of information today with lots of specific recipes and methods of preparation for seaweeds.

We've made some very delicious pickles by taking the "floats" from kelp—the swollen hollow bubble at the base of each frond—and soaking them in jalapeño juice or other pickling juice. They take on the flavor of whatever they are seasoned with.

## CAUTIONS

There are some commonsense precautions you should take if you're going to try some seaweeds. Never eat any seaweed that has been sitting on the beach rotting and attracting flies. Examine the seaweed. Never eat seaweed that has some sort of foreign growth on it. And perhaps the hardest part of all is that you should not consume seaweed from polluted waters. This means that you have to use some common sense when collecting seaweed for food, and you should thoroughly wash any seaweed that you intend to eat.

# Ferns

There are thirteen families of ferns. According to Dr. Leonid Enari, the young, uncurling, growing tips of all ferns are edible, and taste a bit nutty. These have long been steamed and served with butter or cheese, or mixed into various vegetable dishes.

Though Dr. Enari regarded the entire group of ferns as safe for food, he offered the following precautions: Cook all fiddleheads that you intend to eat, since some may be a bit toxic to consume raw. He advised cleaning fiddleheads of hairs, if any, before cooking. Dr. Enari also advised against eating any mature fern fronds. Though many may be safe when mature, they are not as palatable as the young fiddleheads. Thus, you need to get to know that individual fern before you eat its mature fronds. Otherwise, eat only the fiddleheads, clean them of hairs, and cook them before eating.

There are many ferns that you will encounter in Washington and beyond, besides what we have presented here. A few have a long history of use as food.

# BRACKEN FAMILY (Dennstaedtiaceae)

Among the ferns, the Bracken family contains about 11 genera and about 170 species. Its only representative in Washington is the bracken, or brake, fern.

Mature bracken fern RICK ADAMS

## BRACKEN
*Pteridium aquilinum*

**Use:** Young uncurling shoots used for food
**Range:** Throughout the state, mostly in the shady areas of the mountains and canyons; not found in the deserts
**Similarity to toxic species:** See "Cautions."
**Best time:** Spring
**Status:** Somewhat common in the correct terrain
**Tools needed:** Clippers

## PROPERTIES

Bracken can apparently be found worldwide. Ours can be found throughout the state—in pastures, hillsides, wooded areas, and even in full sun. You'll find it most commonly on the north, shady side of hillsides or shady hillsides where water seeps and where little sun gets through the canopy of whatever larger trees grow there.

The rhizomes are hairy and sprawling underground, sometimes branching. The petiole is black near the base, with dense brown hairs. The plants grow 1–4 feet tall, and the overall appearance of each frond is roughly triangular; each is twice-pinnately divided.

## USES

The young shoots are the edible portion, and they have the appearance of the head of a fiddle, hence the common name "fiddlehead." The young shoots will uncurl and grow into the full fern fronds. These are picked when young and can be eaten raw or cooked. I like to toss a few in salads when the fiddleheads are in season; they impart a nutty flavor.

The young tips are used for food.

More commonly, these are boiled or steamed and served with butter or cheese. They are easy to recognize and have gained a resurgence of popularity as more people are rediscovering wild foods. Bracken is also a good vegetable to add to soups and stews and mixed dishes.

Just carefully pinch off the tender unfolding top; you can gently rub off the hair. Use as a nibble or cook. Do not eat the fully opened ferns.

## CAUTIONS

Researchers have identified a substance called ptaquiloside, a known carcinogen, in bracken fern. So is it safe to eat? It has been a food staple of Native Americans for centuries, if not millennia, and the Japanese also enjoy bracken and consider it as one of the delicacies of spring. Although actual scientific data is inconclusive, there is a higher rate of intestinal cancer among Native Americans and the Japanese, and this could be linked to the use of bracken fern. Livestock have been known to be mildly poisoned by eating quantities of the raw

The young fiddlehead RICK ADAMS

bracken ferns. Cooking is known to remove some of the toxins, though not necessarily the ptaquiloside.

Despite this, there are many who are not so concerned about such inconclusive studies. For example, in his *Identifying and Harvesting Edible and Medicinal Plants*, Steven Brill states, "I wouldn't be afraid of eating reasonable quantities of wild [bracken] fiddleheads during their short season." Another forager, Green Deane, says, "I am willing to risk a few fiddleheads with butter once or twice a spring, which is about as often as I can collect enough in this warm place."

The final choice is up to you. For perspective, we regularly hear things far worse than the above about coffee, high-fructose corn syrup, sugar, and french fries, yet people seem to have no problem purchasing and eating these substances. That doesn't make them good for you, but eating some in moderation is not likely to be the sole cause of cancer or other illness.

## LEWIS AND CLARK

Meriwether Lewis wrote about the bracken fern on January 22, 1806:

> There are three species of fern in this neighbourhood the root one of which the natves eat; this grows very abundant in the open uplands and praries . . . the center of the root is divided into two equal parts by a strong flat & white ligament like a piece of thin tape—on either side of this there is a white substance which when the root is roasted in the embers is much like wheat dough and not very unlike it in flavour, though it has also a pungency which becomes more visible after you have chewed it some little time; this pungency was disagreeable to me, but the natives eat it very voraciously and I have no doubt but it is a very nutricious food.

## SOME OTHER FERN GROUPS

The Wood Fern family (Dryopteridaceae) consists of about 40 to 45 genera, 4 local genera, and more than 1,600 species worldwide. This family includes *Dryopteris* spp., consisting of about 100 species worldwide and commonly called wood fern. The family also includes *Polystichum* spp., with about 175 species worldwide and commonly referred to as sword fern.

The Cliff Fern family (Woodsiaceae) consists of 15 genera and about 700 species worldwide. One species sometimes eaten is lady fern (*Athyrium filix-femina*) and two varieties.

The Deer Fern family (Blechnaceae) consists of 9 genera and about 250 species worldwide. Common locally, and sometimes eaten, is deer fern (*Blechnum spicant*).

# Gymnosperms

This is a class of plants whose seeds are formed in cones (as with pine trees) or on stalks (as with the genus *Ephedra*). The members of this group include the cycadophytes, conifers, the ginkgo tree, and the Ephedras.

## PINE FAMILY (Pinaceae)

The Pine family is said to supply about half of the world's lumber needs. The family consists of 10 genera and 193 species. There are ninety-four species of *Pinus* in the Northern Hemisphere, and at least six are known to grow in the wild in Washington.

## PINE
*Pinus* spp.

**Use:** Needles for tea and spice; nuts for food
**Range:** Various species are found in the mountains and throughout the state. Often planted in urban areas.
**Similarity to toxic species:** None
**Best time:** Nuts in the fall; needles can be collected anytime.
**Status:** Common in certain localities
**Tools needed:** Clippers for needles

### PROPERTIES

Pines are fairly widespread trees, with species growing along the coast, in the Cascades, on the eastern slopes, and in bogs, with some preferring burned-over areas. There are ninety-four species in the Northern Hemisphere. In Washington and surrounding area, we find coast pine (*Pinus contorta*), with needles mostly in twos; western yellow pine (*P. ponderosa*), with needles mostly in threes and found mainly in the eastern Cascades; limber pine (*P. flexilis*), with needles in fives, found mostly in the east; whitebark pine (*P. albicaulis*), with needles in fives, found through the Cascades; and western white pine (*P. monticola*), with needles in fives and found in the Olympic Mountains and the Cascades.

Pines are one of the easier conifers to identify: All the needles are "bundled" at their base into groups of one to five with papery sheaths; each such cluster is called a fascicle.

The pines in Washington can range from about 30 feet tall (the coast pine) up to about 200 feet tall (the western yellow pine). You look for the bundled needles and you look for the cones. The cones are often tightly spiraled with a variety of scale types. As the cones mature, they open up to reveal a pine nut under each scale. Each pine nut has a thin black shell and an oily white inside.

FORAGER NOTE: Some of the very long needles of certain pines are excellent for coiled baskets.

## USES

Though there are a few *potential* foods with the pines, it is mostly the seeds that will provide you with food that is both substantial and palatable.

The cones mature and open in the fall. As the scales open sufficiently, the seeds drop to the ground, where they can be collected if you're there at the right time and beat the animals to them. The seeds may drop over a two-week to one-month period. One of the best methods to harvest is to lay sheets under the trees to catch the seeds so they're not lost in the grass. The seeds are then shelled and eaten as a snack, added to soups, or mashed and added to biscuits or pancakes.

I have taken the not-fully-mature cones and put them into the fire, carefully watching them so they don't burn. The idea is to open the scales and then get the seeds. However, I do not recommend this method.

The tender needles can also be collected and brewed into a tea. Put the needles in a covered container and boil at a low temperature for a few minutes. Your tea is vitamin C rich and very aromatic and tasty—that is, if you enjoy the flavor of a Christmas tree, which is what you'll smell like after drinking it. It's very good.

Yes, we have all heard of eating the cambium layer of pine trees. I once read an article titled "Spaghetti That Grows on Trees," and it showed a woman who had peeled off the cambium layer of the bark (the inner layer) and had supposedly cooked strips of it to make a wild spaghetti. She was actually smiling in the picture, which was my clue that she hadn't actually eaten any of this "spaghetti." I regard this as a "survival food," meaning it could be worth all the work involved if you're actually near to starving. You most likely would not break into a smile if you were eating such a fibrous and resinous food.

# Eudicots

This category was formerly referred to as dicots. The sprouts begin with two cotyledons, and the flower parts generally occur in fours or fives. All families in this category are arranged alphabetically by their Latin name.

# MUSKROOT FAMILY (Adoxaceae)

This family has 5 genera and about 200 species worldwide. Only two of the genera are represented in Washington, *Sambucus* and *Viburnum*.

Elder flowers and fruit

## ELDERBERRY
*Sambucus* spp.

There are twenty species of *Sambucus* worldwide and three species in Washington. The blue elderberry, *S. nigra* ssp. *caerulea* (sometimes known as *S. caerulea*), is widespread. The black elderberry, *S. racemosa* var. *melanocarpa*, is also widespread. The red elderberry, *S. racemosa* var. *racemosa* (sometimes known as *S. callicarpa*), is less widespread.

**Use:** Flowers for tea and food; berries for "raisins," jam, jelly, juice
**Range:** Throughout the state in the mountains, urban fringe, and generally most environments
**Similarity to toxic species:** See "Cautions."
**Best time:** Early spring for flowers; early summer for fruit
**Status:** Common
**Tools needed:** Clippers for flowers; clippers and good, sturdy bucket for berries

FORAGER NOTE: If you don't want your fruit to get all smashed and crushed, don't collect in a bag. Collect in a basket or bucket, and don't pack too many into the bucket.

Elder flower cluster

## PROPERTIES

Elder can be found throughout the state—in the drier regions, along streams, and in the higher mountain regions. They are generally small trees, with oppositely arranged, pinnately divided leaves with a terminal leaflet. Each leaflet has a fine serration along its edge.

The plant is often inconspicuous but is very obvious when it blossoms into many yellowish-white flower clusters in the spring. By early summer, the fruits develop in clusters, which are often drooping from the weight.

## USES

Remember this Boy Scout saying about elder: Black and blue is good for you; red as a brick will get you sick!

A bowl of elder fruit

Barbara Kolander collecting some ripe elderberries

The blue berries, rich in vitamin A, with fair amounts of potassium and calcium, can be eaten raw or can be mashed and blended with applesauce for a unique dessert, especially if you are using wild apples. The berries can also be used to make wines, jellies, jams, and pies.

Though some of the Indian tribes of Washington and the Northwest ate the red berries when cooked, there are people today who get sick from them. I do not advise eating red elderberries at all; however, if you decide to try them, cook them well and sample only a little bit at first to see how your body reacts.

Wild-food researcher Pascal Baudar likes to dry and powder the blue fruit and then sprinkle it over ice cream. The whole flower cluster can be gathered, dipped in batter, and fried, producing a wholesome pancake. Try dipping the flower clusters in a batter made with sweet yellow cattail pollen (see "Cattail") and frying it like pancakes. It's delicious!

Another method to use the flowers is to remove them from the clusters and little stems, and then mix with flour in a proportion of 50/50 for baking pastries, breads, biscuits, and more. The flowers also make a traditional Appalachian tea that was said to be useful for colds, fevers, and headaches.

The long, straight stems of elder have a soft pith and have historically been hollowed out and used for such things as pipe stems, blowguns, flutes, and straws for stoking a fire.

## Cautions

Be sure to cook the fruit before eating it, and avoid the red berries entirely. While not everyone will get sick from eating the dark purple or black berries raw, these have caused severe nausea in many people. Therefore, cook all fruit before using for drinks or other dishes. Also, in the beginning, you should only eat these sparingly and with caution.

Do not consume the leaves, as this will result in sickness.

## RECIPE

**Elderberry Sauce**

This simple sauce goes well with any game, such as duck, but feel free to try it with chicken too!

1 pound elderberries (Freeze the clusters first; crush lightly with your hands, and the berries will fall easily.)
1 large sweet onion or 7–8 scallions
⅔ cup red wine vinegar
¾ cup sugar or honey
1 teaspoon grated ginger
A couple of cloves
½ teaspoon salt, or to taste

Place the berries in a pot and squeeze them with your hand to release the juice. Place all the other ingredients in the pot and bring to a boil for 10 minutes, then strain the liquid through a sieve.

Return the liquid to the pot, bring to a simmer, and reduce until you have achieved the right consistency (like a commercial steak sauce). You can prepare the sauce in advance and keep it in the fridge for many days.

—Recipe from Pascal Baudar

# HIGHBUSH CRANBERRY
*Viburnum edule*

There are about 200 species worldwide of *Viburnum*, and at least 3 identified in Washington: *V. edule* (aka *V. opulus* var. *edule*), called squashberry or high-bush cranberry; *V. ellipticum*, or western blackhaw; and *V. opulus* var. *americanum*, also called American bush cranberry or cranberry tree; and *V. opulus* var. *opulus*, also called high-bush cranberry. None of these is related to the common cranberry, which is *Vaccinium macrocarpon*, native to the eastern United States and commonly cultivated.

**Use:** Edible fruits
**Range:** Grows over a broad area on both sides of the Cascades; found from the Pacific to the Atlantic Ocean, and south to northern Oregon. The native species is found in moist woods and swamps.
**Similarity to toxic species:** None
**Best time:** Flowers May to July, with the fruit following in late summer
**Status:** Common
**Tools needed:** A collecting basket

## PROPERTIES

These are deciduous, semi-erect shrubs that can get up to 10 feet tall, but are usually around 4–5 feet tall. The opposite leaves are petiolate, palmately veined, and shallowly three-lobed, appearing somewhat like a currant leaf. Sometimes you'll see some unlobed leaves. Each leaf is sharply toothed, usually 3–10 centimeters long and wide, with a pair of glandular projections near the junction with the petiole. The leaves turn conspicuously red in the fall, and by winter, the leaves fall off. The white flowers are formed in compound umbels. Each corolla is widely bell-shaped, whitish, with five lobes. The fruit is a one-seeded drupe, maturing to a bright red or orange.

Fruit and leaf of *V. opulus* DR. AMADEJ TRNKOCZY

A closer look at the fruit and leaf of *V. opulus* DR. AMADEJ TRNKOCZY

## USES

When you encounter this semi-erect shrub, you will be inclined to taste a fruit if in season. You'll chew on it and spit out the seed, and maybe you'll like it, maybe you won't. I've heard the flavor described as musky; it's a unique flavor. Cooking the fruits to make a jam or jelly will mellow the flavor, and most people will enjoy it at that point. I used to nibble on the raw fruit, but I prefer making a jam or juice from it. I do this by mashing the ripe fruits, pouring the liquid through a sieve, and then gently cooking the juice and sweetening it if I just want a juice. We've also cooked it down and used it as a pie filling.

You could also simply mix the highbush cranberry fruit with other wild or domestic fruits for juices, jams, pie fillings, etc.

Fruits that are left on the bush into the winter will be a bit mellower, and are tasty raw. You might also enjoy drying some of these fruits for later use.

Fruits from the often-cultivated *Viburnum opulus* tend to be more bitter. The native *Viburnum edule* tends to be sweeter.

Another view of the *V. opulus* fruit and leaf ZOYA AKULOVA

# AMARANTH FAMILY (Amaranthaceae)

The Amaranth family has 75 genera and 900 species worldwide. There are about twenty genera of this family in Washington. Of the members of the *Amaranthus* genus in Washington, *A. retroflexus* seems to be the most common of about nine species.

The red root of *A. retroflexus*

## AMARANTH
*Amaranthus* spp.

**Use:** Seeds for soup or pastries and bread products; leaves can be eaten raw or cooked.

**Range:** Amaranth is widespread. Though it is most common in the disturbed soils of farms, gardens, fields, and urban lots, you can usually find some amaranth in open areas where there is some moisture, even seasonally.

**Similarity to toxic species:** Some ornamentals resemble amaranth. Some toxic plants superficially resemble amaranth, such as the nightshades (e.g., *Solanum nigrum*). Individual jimsonweed leaves (*Datura* spp.) have been confused for amaranth leaves. Generally, once the amaranth begins to flower and go to seed, this confusion is diminished.

**Best time:** Spring for the leaves; late fall for the seeds

**Status:** Common

**Tools needed:** Tight-weave bag for collecting the seeds

FORAGER NOTE: Amaranths are a diverse group. Some have an erect stalk, some are highly branched, and some are prostrate.

## PROPERTIES

Though there are many species of *Amaranthus*, *A. retroflexus* is most common in Washington.

Amaranth is an annual. The ones with erect stalks can grow to 3 feet and taller, depending on the species. Some are more branched and are lower to the ground. When young, the root of one of the common varieties, *A. retroflexus*, is red, and the bottoms of the young leaves are purple. The leaves of *A. retroflexus* are oval shaped, alternate, and glossy. Other *Amaranthus* leaves can be ovate to linear.

The plant produces flowers, but they are not conspicuous. They are formed in spikelike clusters, and numerous shiny black seeds develop when the plant matures in late summer. The plant is common and widespread in urban areas, fields, farms, backyards, and roadsides.

## USES

Amaranth is a versatile plant with edible parts available throughout its growing season.

The young leaves and tender stems of late winter and spring can be eaten raw in salads, but because there is often a hint of bitterness, they are best mixed with other greens. Young and tender stems are boiled in many parts of the world and served with butter or cheese as a simple vegetable. Older leaves get bitter and should be boiled into a spinach-like dish or added to soups, stews, stir-fries, etc. In Mexico, leaves are sometimes dried and made into a flour, which is added to tamales and other dishes.

Photographer Rick Adams standing next to an erect amaranth, often cultivated for its seed

*A. retroflexus* plant, also showing the red root
RICK ADAMS

Shiny black seeds from the wild amaranth

Amaranth begins to produce seeds in late summer, and once the seeds are black, they can be harvested. The entire plant is generally already very withered and dried up by the time you're harvesting. The seeds are added to soups, bread batter, and pastry products.

The seeds and leaves are very nutritious, no doubt part of the reason this plant was so revered in the old days. One hundred grams of the seed contains about 358 calories, 247 mg of calcium, 500 mg of phosphorus, and 52.5 mg of potassium. The seed offers a nearly complete balance of essential amino acids, including lysine and methionine.

HISTORICAL NOTE: The seed and leaf of this plant played a key part of the diet in precolonial Mexico. The seeds would be mixed with honey or blood and shaped into images of their gods, and these images were then eaten as a "communion." Sound familiar? After the Spanish invaded Mexico, they made it illegal to grow the amaranth plant, with the justification that it was a part of "pagan rituals."

Young leaves of *Amaranthus retroflexus* RICK ADAMS

The leaf is also very nutritious, being high in calcium and potassium. One hundred grams, about ½ cup, of amaranth leaf has 267–448 mg of calcium, 411–617 mg of potassium, 53–80 mg of vitamin C, 4,300 mcg (micrograms) of beta-carotene, and 1,300 mcg of niacin. This volume of leaf contains about 35 calories.

# CARROT, AKA PARSLEY FAMILY (Apiaceae)

The Carrot family has about 300 genera worldwide, with about 3,000 species. In Washington, there are over thirty genera of this family. Many are cultivated for food, spice, and medicine, but some are highly toxic. Never eat anything that looks carrot- or parsley-like if you haven't positively identified it.

A patch of flowering wild carrots

## WILD CARROT
### Daucus carota

There are about twenty species of *Daucus* worldwide, and two are found in Washington.

**Use:** The root can be dug and used like farm-grown carrots, but they are tougher. Seeds are sometimes used as a spice.

**Range:** Not a native, but can be found throughout much of Washington, often in disturbed or poor soils and along roadsides

**Similarity to toxic species:** See "Cautions."

**Best time:** For a more tender root, dig before the plant flowers.

**Status:** Found sporadically throughout Washington and the Northwest

**Tools needed:** Shovel

The maturing carrot flower typically folds up into a bird's-nest shape.

## PROPERTIES

If you've ever grown carrots in your garden, you will recognize the wild carrot in the wild, except it will typically be smaller. Smell the crushed leaf, and then scrape a bit of the root and smell it. Does it smell like carrot? The root of the wild carrot is white, not orange, and if you scratch it, you'll get that very characteristic and unmistakable carrot aroma.

The leaves are pinnately dissected, with the leaflet segments linear to lanceolate—just like the leaves of a garden carrot. The flowers are formed in umbels of white flowers, with a tiny central flower that is purple. As the umbel matures, it closes up and has the appearance of a bird's nest.

## USES

The roots can be dug, washed, and eaten like garden carrots, though they are usually tough. This was one of the first wild foods that I learned to use. It was always a feeling of great mystery and pleasure to dig into a wild field and pull up one of these white roots. Was it a farm carrot gone feral? Probably. It still woke up some inner distant memory of "hunter-gatherer."

Sometimes I simply peel the outer part of the taproot and discard the very tough inner core. I then wash the outer layer of the root, chop or slice it, and add it to raw or cooked foods.

Note the purple flower in the middle of the carrot inflorescence. ALGIE AU

The root of the wild carrot is a shade of white, not orange. ALGIE AU

The entire root might be tender if it's growing in moist and rich soil. Then it can be sliced thin and added to salads. They're probably best added to soups, stews, and various cooked dishes.

But most of the roots I've found are pretty tough, and only the outer layer can be eaten. I slice this thin and cook it. It adds a good flavor to soups, though it lacks the carotene of commercial carrots.

The seeds of the mature plant can be collected and used as a seasoning, to taste.

FORAGER NOTE: When young, poison hemlock resembles Italian parsley and looks very much like the wild carrot as it grows taller. If uncertain, here are some tips: Rub a leaf and smell the aroma. Does it smell like carrot? Then it probably is. Does it smell musky, like dust or old socks? It's probably poison hemlock. Look at the mature stalk. If you see purple blotches, you have poison hemlock. Look at the flower umbel. Is there a single purple flower in the middle? If so, you have a wild carrot. Remember, never eat any wild plant until you have positively identified it.

This is poison hemlock. Poison hemlock could be confused with wild carrot; however, poison hemlock has purple blotches on the stalk and lacks the conspicuous carrot aroma.

## CAUTIONS

The Carrot family contains some very good food and spices; however, make absolutely certain that you have a carrot and not poison hemlock, which is another member of this family. The wild carrot plant has that very distinctive carrot aroma, and has fine hairs on the stalk. Poison hemlock lacks the hairs, and usually you will see mottled purple markings on the stem.

A simple comparison of wild carrot vs. poison hemlock by Billy Nickel

|  | Wild carrot (*Daucus carota*) | Poison hemlock (*Conium maculatum*) |
|---|---|---|
| Flowers | Flat-topped umbel, with red-purple flower in center. Matures to bird's-nest shape. | Rounded umbel |
| Hairs | Yes | No |
| Leaves | "Ferny," with a hairy underside | Larger, hairless, and shiny |
| Stalk | No purple blotches | Conspicuous purple blotches |
| Aroma | Carrot aroma | Urine aroma |

***Note:*** *Other members of the Carrot/Parsley family might be confused with poison hemlock, such as chervil. Chervil is a much smaller plant, has no blotches, and is hairy; the younger plants only have hair in the crotches. Make sure you positively identify any member of this family before eating it.*—Billy Nickel

Seattle resident Nathaniel Schleimer examines the young shoots of a fennel plant.

## FENNEL
*Foeniculum vulgare*
Fennel is the only species of the *Foeniculum* genus.

**Use:** Leaf and stalk eaten raw or cooked; seed for tea or seasoning
**Range:** Widespread as an "invasive species" along the coast; common locally in urban lots and fields. Well established west of the Cascades.
**Similarity to toxic species:** Fennel has needlelike leaves and smells like licorice, so you really shouldn't confuse it with anything toxic. However, this family contains some poisonous and toxic members, so be certain you're picking fennel before eating it.
**Best time:** Spring for the young shoots; summer or fall for the seeds
**Status:** Widespread and common in certain localities
**Tools needed:** None

## PROPERTIES
Fennel is a perennial from Europe that is very common along the Pacific coast and in wet areas. It is abundant in certain areas and generally considered invasive.

The plant begins to produce its ferny leaves in the spring. The finely dissected leaves—all composed of needlelike segments—give the plant a ferny appearance. The base of each leaf clasps the stalk with a flared base, similar to the base of a celery stalk. The unmistakable characteristic is the strong licorice aroma of the crushed leaf.

The plants begin to appear in winter and early spring. They first establish a ferny, bushy, 2- to 3-foot-broad base. By spring and early summer, the flower stalks rise to a height of 6 feet (higher in ideal conditions). The entire plant has a slightly bluish-green cast due to a thin, waxy coating on the stalks and leaves. The yellow flowers form in large distinctive umbels.

## USES

Young fennel leaves and peeled stalks are great to eat as a trail snack when you're thirsty and hungry. When the plant first sprouts up in the spring, you can eat the entire tender and succulent base, somewhat like you'd eat celery. As it sends up its stalk, but before the plant has flowered, the stalk is still tender and can be easily cut into segments. These tender segments are hollow and round in the cross section and can be used like celery for dipping, or cooked like asparagus and served with cheese and butter.

Later, as the plant grows taller, you can eat the tender leaves and stems, chopped up in salads or added to soups and stews. It gets a bit fibrous as it matures, but can be diced up and added to many dishes. It adds a sweet spiciness to the dishes in which it is used. If you don't care for licorice, you probably won't care for fennel.

When the seeds mature, they can be made into a licorice-flavored tea.

Young fennel plant

Keith Farrar studies a fennel plant. The tan stalks are last year's flower stalks.

Fennel seeds

Just put five or six seeds into a cup and add hot water. The seeds alone can be chewed as a breath freshener or used to season other dishes.

Fennel is widely considered a pest in parts of the Northwest (and because it grows so thick in some areas that it chokes out the native vegetation). However, this is one of those ideal plants to grow in the lazy person's garden. It seems to take care of itself, does well in sun or shade, and continues to arise year after year from its roots, providing seed and leaf for your meals, and perhaps habitat for a few local birds.

Cow parsnip plant in flower BOB SIVINSKI

## COW PARSNIP
*Heracleum maximum,* formerly *H. lanatum*
There are about eighty species of *Heracleum* worldwide; two species are found in Washington.

**Use:** The tender parts of the stalk are edible.
**Range:** Prefers lowlands and moist environments. Can be found in alpine areas.
**Similarity to toxic species:** See "Cautions."
**Best time:** Spring
**Status:** Somewhat common and widespread
**Tools needed:** Knife

## PROPERTIES

This is a robust plant, an obvious member of the Carrot or Parsley family because of the white flowers that are clustered in umbels. The flowers are composed of five sepals, five petals, five stamens, and one pistil.

The plant can grow up to 10 feet tall, though 4–6 feet seems to be the norm. It produces leaves with three large, coarsely toothed lobes, very much palmate, almost like maple leaves. The plant has a stout hollow stalk. There is also a carrot-like taproot.

The plant is most commonly found in mountain meadows and moist areas. It's a conspicuous plant that you cannot help but notice.

Close-up of the cow parsnip stem ZOYA AKULOVA

## USES

The root can be cooked and eaten, with a flavor that has been compared to rutabaga. Herbalists state that eating the root is good for the digestive system.

The tender stalk can be peeled and eaten raw, though it is really better when you cook it. The young stalks are best, and the flavor is often compared to celery.

The dried and powdered leaves have been used as a seasoning for other foods, generally as you'd use salt. You can experiment and see if this appeals to you. The leaves have also been dried and burned, with the ash used as a seasoning.

Native Americans of the area had many uses for the cow parsnip plant besides eating the young peeled stems. They would make the plant into a poultice to treat sores and bruises. The hollow stems were also used as drinking straws, as well as flutes.

## CAUTIONS

Although this is one of the easiest members of the Carrot family to identify, the family does contain some deadly members, so do not eat any part of this plant until you've made positive identification.

Also, the young stalk is typically peeled before eating because the surface of the stalk causes a dermatitis reaction in some people.

Biscuit root plant MARY WINTER

# BISCUIT ROOT
*Lomatium* spp.

There are about seventy-five species of *Lomatium* worldwide. In Washington, there are thirty-two *Lomatium* species; more if you individually count each variety.

**Use:** All parts of the plant are edible, though the roots are most commonly eaten.
**Range:** Widespread in meadows and open slopes. Found on both sides of the Cascades and in the drier interior.
**Similarity to toxic species:** See "Cautions."
**Best time:** Collect roots and leaves in the spring. By summer, the plants typically dry out.
**Status:** Widespread. Can be found up into Canada and south to California.
**Tools needed:** Trowel

## PROPERTIES
These have a taproot that is usually short and tuberous-thickened, irregularly shaped, and occasionally slender and elongate.

The stems tend to be prostrate and creeping, rarely rising much higher than knee high.

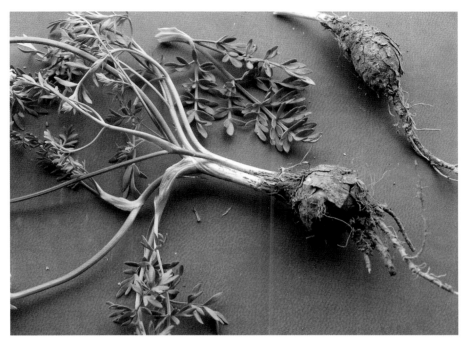
The root of the biscuit root MARY WINTER

Leaves are typically pinnately dissected (or ternately dissected), with the individual leaflets being threadlike to wide. Leaves are usually all basal, but there may be one or more cauline leaves.

Different species can have white, yellow, or purple flowers. Inflorescence is a compound umbel, which matures into seeds with flattened backs and wings.

With a bit of fieldwork, you'll be able to recognize a *Lomatium*, though it may take a bit longer to learn to recognize the different species.

## USES

There are many different species, and the flavor varies. The leaves and the roots can be eaten. The flavor of each will vary with the species, and perhaps with the soil conditions. Sometimes they taste very "medicinal," and sometimes the flavor is good, almost sweet.

While the root can be eaten raw, it will be more tender and taste better if cooked. The smaller, younger roots are generally tastier and more tender. Native people would crush the roots into a flour, which was then boiled, steamed, or roasted. It was then dried and reconstituted later, or used as a trade item (see "Lewis and Clark"). Slower cooking is considered the best way to bring out the sweeter flavor of the roots.

While these roots were one of the most important Native foods (along with camas), not everyone finds the flavor agreeable. Everyone's sense of taste is different, and different soils in different eco-zones will affect the quality of the plants growing there. Remember, if you don't like it, don't eat it! On the other hand, I have discovered that after around three days of no food, just about any "edible" plant will start to taste quite toothsome.

These leaves are often the first leaves of late winter or spring that you can collect in sagebrush country. The leaves vary in flavor, sometimes described as celery-like. They are best collected in the spring, and can be used raw or cooked.

The little seeds are best if collected before the plant begins to dry up. These can be added to other foods as a spice.

## CAUTIONS

Because the deadly poison hemlock and water hemlock are in this same family, with the same floral structure, you must be absolutely certain you are identifying biscuit root if you intend to eat it. There are several significant differences between biscuit root and poison hemlock. Poison hemlock can grow to 7 feet tall, with stout hollow stems that are blotched with purple as it matures. There is really no way that an observant forager would confuse poison hemlock for biscuit root, or any *Lomatium* species for that matter.

## LEWIS AND CLARK

This was one of the most important plants for Native Americans of the upper Columbia River drainage. Speaking of *Lomatium cous*, known as "cous" or "cows," Lewis wrote what he observed by the Nez Perce, then called Chopunnish.

On May 9, 1806, Lewis wrote:

> [A]mong other roots those called by them the Quawmash [camas] and Cows [Cous Bisquitroot] are esteemed the most agreeable and valuable as they are also the most abundant. The cows is a knobbed root of an irregularly rounded form not unlike the Gensang [American ginseng] in form and consistence. This root they collect, rub of a thin black rhind which covers it and pounding it expose it in cakes to the sun. These [cous] cakes ate [at] about an inch and ¼ thick and 6 by 18 in width, when dryed they either eat this bread alone without any further preparation, or boil it and make a thick muselage; the latter is most common and much the most agreeable. The flavor of this root is not very unlike the gensang—this [cous] root they collect as early as the snows disappear in the spring.

Later, Lewis related how a captain was given some dried camas roots as a present. Lewis wrote: "[B]ut in our estimation those of cows (*Lomatium cous*) are much better, I am confident they are much more healthy. The men . . . obtained a good store of roots and bread."

Flowering yampa plant in the field MARGO BORS

## YAMPA
*Perideridia gairdneri,* formerly *P. montana*
There are about a dozen species of *Perideridia* worldwide, and three of them are found in Washington.

**Use:** All parts of the plant are edible, though the roots are most commonly eaten.
**Range:** Widespread, most often in grassy meadows
**Similarity to toxic species:** See "Cautions."
**Best time:** For a more-tender root, dig the roots in the spring. Seeds can be gathered in autumn.
**Status:** Widespread, mostly in the eastern part of the state. Can be found up into Canada, east beyond Idaho, and south to Colorado.
**Tools needed:** Trowel

Yampa roots TOM ELPEL

A closer view of the yampa flower TOM ELPEL

## PROPERTIES

This is a perennial, growing around 2 to 3½ feet tall. It's an obvious member of the Parsley family, with its white flowers in compound umbels that typically appear in July and August. The narrow linear segments of the leaves are pinnately divided, or ternate-pinnately compound. Leaves are from 1 to 12 inches long, which is quite a range, but it all depends on the soil conditions in which they're growing. They appear almost grasslike, blending in well with the grass so they are hardly noticed until they flower. The root is small, somewhat rounded at one end and coming to a point at the other end. Often the roots are formed in pairs.

## USES

When the leaves are tender, they can be added to salads and used as a nibble. The flowers can likewise be used in salads or in cooked dishes.

However, the small roots are the most desirable part of this plant, tasty both raw and cooked. The raw roots have a nutty flavor, like a water chestnut, and also reminiscent of a spicy carrot. These can be chopped into salads or just used as a snack. They are mild and tasty when baked or boiled, and you'll find that no one rejects this pleasant food. Their small size, however, means you'll be putting in your work to get enough for a meal. Tom Elpel, in his *Foraging the Mountain West* books, describes that it takes him about an hour with a digging stick to harvest just a cup of the roots.

## CAUTIONS

Because the deadly poison hemlock is in this family and therefore has the same floral structure, you must be absolutely certain you are identifying yampa if you intend to eat it. There are several significant differences between yampa and poison hemlock. Poison hemlock can grow to 7 feet tall, with stout hollow stems that are blotched with purple as it matures. There is really no way an observant forager would confuse poison hemlock for yampa.

Also, be a conscientious forager. Loosen the soil so you can remove the largest roots, but return the smaller ones back to the soil for the following years.

## LEWIS AND CLARK

On August 26, 1805, in next-door Idaho, Lewis wrote the following description of yampa, which he called "fennel":

> I observe the Indian women collecting the root of a speceis of fennel which grows in the moist grounds and feeding their poor starved children. . . . The radix [the root] of this plant is of the knob kind, of a long ovate form terminating in a single radicle [root], the whole bing ["being"] about 3 or 4 inches in length and the thickest part about the size of a man's little finger. It is white firm and crisp in its present state, when dried and pounded it makes a fine white meal; the flavor of this root is not unlike that of annis-seed but not so pungent; the stem rises to the hight of 3 or 4 feet is jointed smooth and cilindric; from 1 to 4 of those knobed roots are attached to the base of this stem. The leaf is sheathing sessile [no stalk to the leaf] . . . the divisions long and narrow; the whole is of a deep green. It is now in blume; the flowers are numerous, small, petals white, and are arranged in the umbellaferous kind.

On May 18, 1806, Lewis described how he observed Sacagawea collecting a store of the yampa roots for the Rocky Mountains. Lewis stated that the Shoshone called this root the "year-pah."

# SUNFLOWER FAMILY (Asteraceae)

Worldwide, the Sunflower family has about 1,500 genera and about 23,000 species! This is the largest family in Washington.

Jepson divides this very large family into fourteen groups. Most of the plants addressed here are in Group 7, described as having ligulate heads, five-lobed ligules (five teeth per petal), and generally containing milky sap when broken. When I was studying botany in the 1970s, my teachers described this group as "the Chicory Tribe," a much more descriptive title than the unimaginative "Group 7." According to Dr. Leonid Enari, the Chicory Tribe contains no poisonous members and is a worthy group for further edibility research. I have eaten many of the other members of this group not listed here, though generally they require extensive boiling and water changing to render edible and palatable.

## GROUP 4

## BURDOCK
*Arctium minus* and *A. lappa*
There are ten species of *Arctium* throughout Europe, and two are found in Washington.

A first-year burdock leaf

**Use:** The root, stems, and leaves can be eaten.

**Range:** Not a native, but can be found throughout the state. Prefers old orchards, waste areas, and fields.

**Similarity to toxic species:** Resembles a rhubarb leaf

**Best time:** Best time to dig the root is in the first year's growth.

**Status:** Relatively common

**Tools needed:** Shovel

## PROPERTIES

The first time I saw wild burdock, I thought I was looking at a rhubarb plant, though the stalk was not red and celery-like, as with rhubarb.

The first-year plant produces a rosette of rhubarb-type leaves; in ideal soil, the second-year plant produces the flowers and burs on a stalk that can rise from 6 to 9 feet tall. Both of these species are similar, with *A. lappa* growing a bit taller.

The leaves are heart shaped (cordate) or broadly ovate and conspicuously veined. The first-year leaves are large and up to 2 feet in length. In the second season, the plant sends up a flower stalk with similar, but smaller, leaves. The purple to white flowers, compressed in bur-like heads, bloom in July and August. The seed containers are spiny-hooked burs that stick to socks and pants.

Burdock seed capsules JEAN PAWEK

The root is sliced and made ready for cooking.

Burdock's root looks like an elongated carrot, except that it is white inside with a brownish-gray skin that is peeled away before eating. You sometimes find this root in markets, sold as "gobo."

## USES

Though you could use all parts of this plant, it is the roots that everyone seeks.

The first-year roots can be dug, washed, and eaten once peeled. They are usually simmered in water until tender and cooked with other vegetables. In Russia, the roots have been used as potato substitutes when potatoes aren't available. Roots can be peeled and sliced into thin pieces and sautéed or cooked with vegetables. I also eat young tender roots diced into a salad and find them very tasty.

Leaves can be eaten once boiled; in some cases, two boilings are necessary, depending on your taste. Try to get them very young. Peeled leaf stems can be eaten raw or cooked. The erect flower stalks, collected before the flowers open, can be peeled of their bitter green skin and then dried or cooked, though these tend to be much more fibrous than the leaf stems.

An analysis of the root (100 g or ½ cup) shows 50 mg of calcium, 58 mg of phosphorus, and 180 mg of potassium. Tea of the roots is said to be useful in treating rheumatism.

A first-year burdock plant in the field LOUIS-M. LANDRY

Herbalists all over the world use burdock: The roots and seeds are a soothing demulcent, tonic, and alterative (restorative to normal health). According to Linda Sheer, who grew up in rural Kentucky, burdock leaf was the best herbal treatment her people used for rattlesnake bites. Two leaves are simmered in milk and given to the victim to drink. The burdock helps counteract the effects of the venom. The body experiences both shock and calcium loss as a result of a rattlesnake bite. The lactose in the burdock milk offsets the calcium loss and prevents or reduces shock. (***Note:*** Seeking professional care and administration of antivenin is recommended for any venomous snakebite.)

You can also take the large burdock leaves and wrap fish and game in them before roasting in the coals of a fire pit. Foods cooked this way are mildly seasoned by the leaves.

# THISTLE
*Cirsium* spp.
Worldwide, there are about 200 species of the *Cirsium* genus. At least eleven are found in Washington, not including varieties.

**Use:** Edible stems, youngest leaves
**Range:** Found throughout the state in most areas
**Similarity to toxic species:** None
**Best time:** Spring
**Status:** Widespread
**Tools needed:** Knife, clippers, bag

## PROPERTIES
There are many species of thistle, all with very similar appearances. Thistles normally reach 4–5 feet at maturity. They can be either perennial or biennial herbs.

Thistle leaves are alternate leaves, prickly or spiny, and generally toothed. They're about 8 inches long at maturity. Thistle flowers are clustered in bristly heads. They are crimson, purple, pink, and occasionally white. The lower half of the flower head is covered with spiny bracts, resembling its cultivated relative, the artichoke.

## USES
When the plant is young and no flower stalk has emerged, the root can be dug, boiled, and eaten. These are starchy roots, mild flavored; as the plant flowers, the root becomes tough and fibrous. If you want to try eating the roots, you want to search in the spring in rich soil. If the soil and timing are not right, the root will be too tough to eat.

Young thistle rosette

Showy thistle flower RICK ADAMS

My favorite part of the thistle is the stalk, cut before the flowers develop, while the stalk is still tender and perhaps about 3 feet tall. Using a sharp knife, I first cut off the bristly leaves and then carefully scrape off the spiny outer layer on the stalk so I can handle it. Once the stalk is scraped of its outer fibrous layer, you can eat it raw—it is sweet and somewhat reminiscent of celery. We've served it with peanut butter for a tasty snack.

These cleaned stalks can be baked, boiled, sautéed, or added to other foods. They also can be served with butter or cheese, as you might serve asparagus.

If you've ever seen a garden artichoke, then the relationship of artichoke to thistle might be obvious. Can you eat the flowering head of the thistle like you can an artichoke? Well, it depends. First, you have to clip the thistle flower while it's still young, and before it has actually flowered. You boil it, and then if you peel back all the scaly bracts, you'll find just a little bit of the tender heart there. It's very tasty, and worth trying, but usually there is really not that much heart to the wild thistle to make it worth your bother.

In general, I don't eat the leaves because I find the prickliness irritating. However, if you can find the very youngest growth of spring, you can collect some very tasty greens that would even be good in a salad. On occasion, when the timing was right, I was able to collect many of the very young emerging cotyledons and add them to salads and cooked dishes.

Low-growing pineapple weed in the field

## PINEAPPLE WEED
*Matricaria discoidea,* formerly *M. matricarioides*
There are seven species of *Matricaria* worldwide, with two found in Washington.

**Use:** The entire plant can be used for a pleasant tea.
**Range:** Widespread, preferring hard soils
**Similarity to toxic species:** Superficially resembles very young poison hemlock
**Best time:** Spring, when the flowers are present
**Status:** Prefers hard-packed soils
**Tools needed:** Sharp knife or scissors, bag

### PROPERTIES
This is a relative of the chamomile plant, so if you've ever grown chamomile, you have a good idea of the general appearance of pineapple weed. Still, chamomile and pineapple weed are not synonymous. Chamomile flowers have white petals, and pineapple weed lacks petals.

Close-up of the pineapple weed plant

Most commonly, pineapple weed is found growing in rock-hard soil, maybe where cars have driven—the type of soil where you cannot easily stick a shovel.

This is an annual herb that can arise as much as 8 inches but is usually less than that—typically 3 or 4 inches tall. The leaves are finely divided into short, narrow linear segments, which are alternately arranged and glabrous (not hairy). The flower heads are formed at the ends or tips of the branches and are cone shaped and small, about ½ inch in length. There are no ray flowers on the pineapple weed, meaning no petals.

When you crush the leaves, and particularly the greenish flower head, you get a distinctive aroma of pineapple, hence the name. Some will find the aroma suggestive of common chamomile.

## USES

I have had the young heads served as a garnish in salads, and even tossed into soups. But most of the time, the plant is used to make a pleasant beverage. Pineapple weed is closely related to chamomile, but according to Dr. Enari, its active chemistry is a bit weaker than chamomile. Still, it is used medicinally in all the ways you'd use chamomile, such as for its calming effect. Additionally, many people use it as a beverage simply because they enjoy its flavor.

The whole aboveground herb can be cut and infused to make a pleasant tea. Or you can snip off just the flowers to make an even more flavorful beverage. Some people find the flavor of the entire herb a bit bitter, so we can say this is an acquired taste. If you want to take the time, you can just pick the flowers and brew them; this doesn't have the bitterness you'll find with the leaf.

Pineapple weed sometimes grows in thick patches.

You can dry this herb for later out-of-season use, or you can use it fresh when in season. Drink plain or sweetened, as you wish.

## CAUTIONS

Since these low-growing plants are so close to the ground, be sure to wash them well before using.

A patch of chicory in flower RICK ADAMS

## GROUP 7
(or Group 8, depending on which botanist you follow)
Heads ligulate, ligules five-lobed, generally white sap present.

## CHICORY
*Cichorium intybus*
There are about six species of *Cichorium* worldwide; only this one is found in Washington. You can occasionally find the related endive, which is not common, near gardens or farms where it has gone wild.

**Use:** Root for beverage and food; greens raw or cooked
**Range:** Widespread; found especially in the disturbed soils of farms, fields, and gardens
**Similarity to toxic species:** None
**Best time:** Spring
**Status:** Common locally
**Tools needed:** Digging tool for digging roots

The sky-blue chicory flower RICK ADAMS

## PROPERTIES

The chicory plant grows upright, typically 3–5 feet tall, with its beautiful and prominent sky-blue flowers. Look carefully at the flower—each petal is divided into five teeth, typical of the Chicory Tribe of the Sunflower family. Each leaf will produce a bit of milky sap when cut. The older upper leaves on the stalk very characteristically clasp the stem at the base.

This is a perennial from Europe that is now widespread in parts of Washington, mostly in fields, gardens, disturbed soils, and along roadsides.

## USES

This is another of those incredibly nutritious plants with multiple uses. The leaves can be added to salads, preferably the very young leaves. If you don't mind a bit of bitterness, the older leaves can be added to salads too. The leaves can be cooked like spinach and added to a variety of dishes, such as soups, stews, and egg dishes.

Chicory roots are also used, either boiled and buttered or sliced and added to stews and soups. Roots in rich soil tend to be less woody and fibrous.

Chicory roots have long been used as a substitute for coffee or as a coffee extender. Dig and wash the roots; then dry them, grind them, and roast them

Flowering chicory plant RICK ADAMS

until they are brown. Use as you would regular coffee grounds, alone or as a coffee extender. Incidentally, you can make this same coffee substitute/extender with the roots of dandelion and sow thistle.

***Note:*** The entire Chicory Tribe of the Sunflower family contains no poisonous members, though many are bitter. These are generally tender-leaved plants with milky sap and "dandelion-like" flowers, each petal of which usually has five teeth at the tip.

Young rosettes of cat's ear

## CAT'S EAR
*Hypochaeris radicata*
There are about sixty species of *Hypochaeris* worldwide, with just two found in Washington: this one, also known as "rough cat's ear," and *H. glabra*, or "smooth cat's ear."

**Use:** Leaves and shoots eaten
**Range:** This plant likes lawns and fields, and is found in the same environments as dandelion.
**Similarity to toxic species:** Though this can be easily confused with other species when not in flower, none are toxic.
**Best time:** Spring
**Status:** Widespread through the state; more common west of the Cascades
**Tools needed:** Collecting bag

### PROPERTIES
When seen for the first time, most folks think they are looking at a dandelion, though it's not quite a dandelion. Yes, cat's ear is found in pretty much the same environments as dandelion: lawns, fields, along trails, and in disturbed soils. I've

seen whole lawns covered in just this plant.

The plant will grow into a rosette of dandelion-like leaves. In some cases, the leaves more closely resemble prickly lettuce. However, the lobes of cat's ear leaves are not sharply defined as with dandelion; rather, they are somewhat rounded, as you can see in the photo. The leaves of cat's ear are also a bit tougher than dandelion, almost leathery in some cases.

The flower stalk arises very much dandelion-style, with a similar composite flower. Because this plant is a member of the Chicory Tribe of the Sunflower family, you will see slight milkiness when you break the stem, in addition to the five tiny teeth at the tip of each yellow flower petal.

Cat's ear plant in flower

## USES

The young leaves can be added to various raw or cooked dishes. However, for salads, only the very youngest leaves should be used, as the leaves develop a toughness as they mature. The raw leaves are bitter, but not terribly so, and are best mixed with other greens.

Many leaves can be collected, then washed and used as a spinach dish. They are okay cooked alone but are much better when mixed with other greens and vegetables.

John Kallas, author of *Edible Wild Plants*, describes collecting

Close-up of the cat's ear leaf

Cat's ear in flower, with a human perspective

the young tender shoots, about 3–4 inches. He steams these and serves them like asparagus, though they are not as tender. In fact, a plate of cat's ear shoots looks very much like a plate of asparagus. You can then serve them with your favorite sauce, or try topping them with butter or cheese.

A rosette of the young prickly lettuce plant, when it could still be used in a salad

## PRICKLY LETTUCE
*Lactuca serriola* and others

There are about one hundred species of *Lactuca* worldwide, with at least seven found in Washington. *Lactuca serriola*, a European native, is probably the most abundant and widespread.

**Use:** Young leaves, raw or cooked
**Range:** Most commonly found in gardens, disturbed soils, along trails, and edges of farms
**Similarity to toxic species:** None
**Best time:** Early spring
**Status:** Widespread

FORAGER NOTE: One of the common names for this plant is "compass plant." When the plant is mature, the edges of the leaves tend to point toward the sun as the sun moves across the sky. This is probably a mechanism to stop water loss. While this is by no means as accurate as using a compass, it could help you determine directions with a bit of figuring.

## PROPERTIES

Prickly lettuce is a very common annual plant that you can find just about anywhere, hidden in plain view. Yes, you've seen it, but it likely blended into the landscape. It's mostly an "urban weed," though occasionally you'll find it in the "near wilderness" surrounding urban areas.

Prickly lettuce rises with its erect stalk to generally no more than 3 feet. The young leaves are lanceolate with generally rounded ends. They are tender, and if you tear a leaf, you'll see white sap. The plant grows upright with an erect stem, which develops soft spines as it gets older. As the plant matures, you'll note that there is a stiff line of hairs on the bottom midrib of the leaf. The leaf attachment is either sessile or clasping the stem, and the leaf shape can be quite variable, from a simple oblong-lanceolate leaf to one that is divided into pinnately lobed segments. Despite this, after you've seen a few prickly lettuce plants, you should readily recognize it.

Ben Hererra examines a prickly lettuce plant during spring.

This shows why you don't eat mature prickly lettuce leaves.

The flowers are small and dandelion-like, pale yellow, with about a dozen ray flowers per head. As with dandelion, these mature into small seeds attached to a little cottony tuft.

## USES

Prickly lettuce sounds like something you'd really like in a salad, but in fact you need to find the very youngest leaves, before they get too tough and bitter. Very young leaves (before the plant has sent up its flower stalk) are good added to your salads and sandwiches. The leaves can also be collected and mixed into stir-fries or added to soups or any sort of stew to which you would add wild greens.

But let's not be fooled by the name "lettuce." Yes, it's botanically a relative of the cultivar you buy in the supermarket, but the leaves become significantly bitter as they age, and the rib on the underside of each older leaf develops stiff spines that make any similarity to lettuce very distant. This means you'll be using this plant raw only when it's very young; when it's flowering and mature, you probably won't be using it at all.

Erect stalk of the prickly lettuce plant

Still, it's edible, and it grows everywhere. You should get to know this plant, and its relatives, and learn to recognize it early in the growing season.

I've used it when *very* young in sandwiches, salads, soups, stews, and egg dishes. I've even used the small root when I was experimenting with coffee substitutes. Since prickly lettuce is related to dandelion and sow thistle, I figured it would work well as a coffee substitute. It does, but there's very little root to this plant.

Nipplewort flower and leaf

## NIPPLEWORT
*Lapsana communis*
Not all botanists agree on this one, but there are believed to be nine species of *Lapsana* worldwide. Only this species is found in Washington.

**Use:** Entire plant can be eaten.
**Range:** Found throughout the state
**Similarity to toxic species:** None
**Best time:** Spring
**Status:** Somewhat common
**Tools needed:** Container for collecting

### PROPERTIES
This European annual or biennial is a member of the Sunflower family. The plants begin with a basal rosette of leaves. As the plant matures, each leaf has a large end lobe, a bit pointed, with smaller lobes. Though closely

Nipplewort plant In flower LOUIS-M. LANDRY

related to sow thistle, the appearance is more of a mustard leaf. The upper surface of each leaf is covered in short, tiny hairs.

The leaf stem is triangular in its cross section, though it is very much like celery where it is attached to the main stem. As the flower stalk develops, the leaves that form on the stalk are smaller and narrower.

Flower buds are formed at the tips of the branching stem, and they are smaller, generally less than ¼ inch long. Yellow dandelion-like flowers develop, with eight bracts surrounding each bud. There are five teeth at the end of each petal, just like every other member of the Chicory Tribe.

Nipplewort flower LOUIS-M. LANDRY

## USES

The leaves are best collected when the plant is young, and steaming or boiling is probably the best way to produce the tastiest and most palatable spinach-like dish. You can add nipplewort to soups, stews, and omelets, or just have it boiled alone and seasoned to taste.

The leaves can be used in salads and are best if mixed with other greens. When chopped and mixed with other greens, the tiny hairs are not noticeable, but if you try to serve a salad of only nipplewort, you're likely to notice the hairs, just as you would with a salad of wild radish greens.

You're going to use this plant very much in the same way that you use sow thistle in cooked dishes.

Individual nipplewort leaf LOUIS-M. LANDRY

Maturing sow thistle plant

## SOW THISTLE
*Sonchus oleraceus* and others
There are about fifty-five species of *Sonchus* worldwide. Four are found in Washington, all of which are from Europe and are edible.

**Use:** Mostly the leaves, raw or cooked; root can be cooked and eaten; flower buds can be pickled.
**Range:** Most common in urban areas, gardens, and farms, but can be found in most environments
**Similarity to toxic species:** None
**Best time:** Spring, though the older leaves of late summer are still useful.
**Status:** Common
**Tools needed:** Trowel for digging

## PROPERTIES

Though the common sow thistle (*S. oleraceus*) is most commonly used for food, the other three species found in Washington look very similar and can be used the same way. When you see *S. asper*, the prickly sow thistle, you may conclude that it's too much work to use for a dish

FORAGER NOTE: Sow thistle is one of our most common wild foods. It is so widespread that it can be found in nearly every environment, even the cracks of urban sidewalks.

of cooked greens because it is covered with soft spines.

When most people see a flowering common sow thistle for the first time, they think it's a dandelion. Yes, it is related to the dandelion, and, yes, the flowers are very similar.

Here is a simple distinction: All dandelion leaves arise directly from the taproot, forming a basal rosette. Sow thistle sends up a much taller stalk, up to 5 feet or so in ideal conditions but usually about 3 feet. The leaves are formed along this more or less erect and branching stalk. The leaves are paler and more tender than dandelion leaves, and sow thistle leaves are not as jagged on the edges as dandelion. And though the individual dandelion and sow thistle flowers are very similar, dandelion only forms one flower per stalk, whereas sow thistle forms many flowers per stalk.

## USES

Though sow thistle may not be quite as nutritious as dandelion, it's definitely tastier and the leaves are more tender. You can include the leaves of sow thistle in salads, and even when the plant is old, there is only a hint of bitterness. The flavor and texture are very much like the lettuce you might grow in your garden.

Ben Hererra examines the multiple flowers on a tall sow thistle plant.

The leaves and tender stems are also ideally added to soups and stews, or simply cooked up by themselves and served like spinach greens. They are tasty alone, or you can try different seasonings (peppers, butter, and cheese) that you enjoy.

The root can be eaten or made into a coffee substitute, as is commonly done with two of its relatives, dandelion and chicory. To eat the roots, gather the young ones and boil till tender. Season as you wish, and serve. The roots could also be washed and added to soups and stews.

For a coffee substitute, gather and wash the roots, then dry thoroughly. Grind them into a coarse meal, roast to a light shade of brown, and then percolate into a caffeine-free beverage. Is it "good"? It's all a matter of personal preference.

Sow thistle at a prime stage for eating. All of the tender portions can be eaten.

## RECIPE

**Spring Awakening**

For a dish that resembles asparagus, take just the tender sow thistle stems in springtime (the leaves can be removed and added to other dishes). Boil or steam the stems until tender—it doesn't take long—and then lay on your plate like asparagus. Add some cheese or butter; it will make a delicious dish, but one you'll only enjoy in the spring—timing is everything.

Flower arising from the young rosette of dandelion

## DANDELION
*Taraxacum officinale*
There are about sixty species of *Taraxacum* worldwide, with at least three of these found in Washington.

**Use:** Leaves raw or cooked; root cooked or processed into a beverage
**Range:** Prefers lawns and fields; disturbed soils
**Similarity to toxic species:** None
**Best time:** Spring for the greens; anytime for the roots
**Status:** Common
**Tools needed:** Trowel for the roots

### PROPERTIES
Even people who say they don't know how to identify any plants can probably identify a dandelion in a field. The characteristic yellow composite flower sits atop the narrow stem, which arises directly from the taproot. There is one yellow flower per flower stalk. These mature into the round, puffy seed heads that children like to blow on and make a wish.

Dandelions grow in fields, lawns, vacant lots, and along trails. They tend to prefer disturbed soils, though I have seen them in the wilderness.

The leaves are dark green, toothed on the margins, and each arises from the root. The name "dandelion" actually comes from the French *dent-de-leon*, meaning "tooth of the lion," for the jagged edges of the leaves.

## USES

My first exposure to dandelion was at about age seven, when my father would pay me a nickel to dig them out of our front yard lawn and throw them in the trash. Boy, things have changed! These days, I would not consider having a front lawn, and I definitely would not dig out the dandelions and toss them in the trash.

Dandelion is another versatile wild food. It's not native to Washington, but is now found all over the world. The yellow flowers make the plant conspicuous in fields and lawns, though it's really the leaves and root that are most used by the forager.

If you want raw dandelion greens, you'll want to pick them as early as possible in the season, before they become bitter. The bitterness is not bad, and it can be mellowed out by adding other greens. Also, an oil-rich dressing makes a dandelion salad more palatable.

It's understandable that dandelions have gotten more popular—they are, after all, the richest source of beta-carotene, even more so than carrots. However, not all the greens sold as "dandelion" in farmers' markets and supermarkets are the genuine leaf. We frequently see various endive relatives sold and called "dandelion."

Dandelion root

Dandelion plant with a mature seed head

Young rosette of dandelion

The roots are also edible. The younger roots, and plants growing in rich soil, are more tender and more desirable. But I have eaten old roots and tough roots and have found a way to make them palatable. Generally I scrub the roots to get rid of all the soil, and then boil until tender. You can boil them whole or slice them and, when tender, use in stews and soups.

For a "coffee-substitute" beverage, wash and then dry the roots. Though there are a few ways you can do this, I generally do a coarse grind and then roast them in the oven until they are mildly brown. Then I do a fine grind and percolate them into a beverage. You can drink it "black" or add honey and cream.

Round seed head of salsify and flowers

## SALSIFY
*Tragopogon* spp.

There are about forty-five species of *Tragopogon* worldwide. Six have been identified in Washington, having either yellow or purple flowers. All are introduced.

**Use:** The root is used most commonly; the tender leaves can also be eaten.

**Range:** Widespread in lower elevations, along roadsides, hillsides, and in developed areas

**Similarity to toxic species:** None

**Best time:** Roots are best gathered in the spring; greens can be collected anytime, but are best in spring.

**Status:** Relatively common

**Tools needed:** Shovel

### PROPERTIES

This is a fairly widespread and easy to recognize plant. Most folks initially notice the large dandelion-like flower, except it is on a much taller stalk, perhaps 2 feet or so tall. Depending on the species, the flower may be yellow or purple, and it will have noticeable bracts that extend beyond

First-year salsify plant

Salsify flower

the petals. The seed head is just like the dandelion seed head, but bigger and very round, around 4 inches diameter. The leaves are linear, almost grasslike, and will exude a milky sap (like dandelion or sow thistle) when broken.

Salsify is a biennial plant, meaning that it produces leaves in the first year; in the second year, it sends up its flower stalk before it dies. The roots of the first-year plant are the most tender. If you pick the root from a flowering plant, it will be tough and a bit bitter. These are sometimes cultivated and, in those cases, are likely to produce larger and more tender roots. But in the wild, the roots you're likely to find are thin, like pencils.

## USES

Salsify, also called oyster plant, is most often used for the root. Before I ever ate one, I read the descriptions of "large fleshy roots" with an oyster flavor, and imagined something like a carrot or radish that would cook up into some exotic seafood-like dish. However, the reality is a little different. Most of the time I find the plant growing in compacted and hard soil, so the root never had a chance to get large and fleshy. It is more like a slender carrot, a bit fibrous, and though the flavor is somewhat bland, the texture is improved by cooking.

Of course, it didn't help that when I was first digging up the salsify roots, they were all from the flowering plants, because those were the ones that I recognized as salsify. But these were the older, second-year plants with tougher roots.

Yes, there are cases where you will find an easy-to-dig root that is pretty darn good, such as during the rainy season in mulchy soil. Either way, this is such a

Just-harvested first-year salsify root

common plant that you should at least try it. And because it's an introduced exotic, no one will mind if you do some volunteer weed removal.

Try cooking it to tenderize, and then slice the root and add to soups and stews. Does it really taste like oyster? Maybe, maybe not. Perhaps there is a slight flavor reminiscent of something like oyster.

We have also cooked up the entire aboveground plant and eaten all that was tender. The stalk will usually be tough, but the leaves are tasty and chewy.

When doing underground pit cooking, we have covered potatoes and onions and meat with the upper part of the salsify plant, which was abundant. Not only did these leaves protect the vegetables we were steaming, but we found these greens to be a tasty addition to our meal as well.

Arrowleaf balsamroot BARRY BRECKLING

## ARROWLEAF BALSAMROOT
*Balsamorhiza sagittata*
There are ten recorded species of *Balsamorhiza*, all of which can be found in Washington. *B. sagittata* seems to have been used the most, along with *B. deltoidea*.

**Use:** All parts can be used for food, though the root is the most desirable.
**Range:** Widespread east of the Cascades, often in rocky and dry soils
**Similarity to toxic species:** None
**Best time:** Roots are best gathered in the spring; greens can be collected anytime, but are best in spring.
**Status:** Relatively common
**Tools needed:** Shovel

## PROPERTIES

This is a somewhat conspicuous perennial, with its large arrow-head-shaped leaves. The leaves are covered with soft hairs, giving the leaf a pale green to whitish cast. The typical Sunflower family flowers are solitary on the long (about 1½ feet) leafless stalk. Each petal is yellow.

The taproot is shaped somewhat like a carrot.

## USES

The greens are best if gathered in the spring and summer. The flavor varies, often described as a citrus flavor. The best leaves are collected from the young plants. The leaves and stems can be eaten raw or cooked into stews, soups, or mixed greens. Cooking mellows both the flavor and the texture.

Arrowleaf balsamroot

A few of the foragers I spoke to said they enjoyed the leaves and stems—mostly cooked. A few others said the plant is "barely palatable." The leaf and flower stems are best if used only in the early spring; if collected too late, they become tough, bitter, and aromatic, and you'd not likely include them in any dish.

The roots were of great importance to the Northwest tribes, who often used them in great numbers. They can be eaten raw, but they become especially flavorful when baked or boiled.

## LEWIS AND CLARK

Clark collected a specimen on April 14, 1806, above the mouth of the White Salmon River, which he called "Canoe Creek." Frederick Pursh recorded: "The stem is eaten by the natives, without any preparation." Clark wrote on the same day: "After dinner we proceeded on our voyage. I walked on Shore with Shabono on the N.Side through a handsome bottom. Met several parties of women and boys in Serch of herbs & roots to Subsist on maney of them had parcels of the Stems of the Sun flower . . . ," referring to arrowleaf balsamroot.

# BARBERRY FAMILY (Berberidaceae)

The Barberry family consists of about 16 genera and approximately 670 species worldwide. Only three of these genera are found in Washington.

Leaf and fruit of Oregon grape

## OREGON GRAPE, aka BARBERRY
*Berberis aquifolium,* formerly *Mahonia aquifolium*

The fruits of all members of the *Berberis* genus are edible. There are approximately 600 species of *Berberis* worldwide. In Washington, you'll find common Oregon grape (*B. aquifolium*), mountain Oregon grape (*B. nervosa*), and four other species.

**Use:** Fruits eaten raw or made into wine, jams, or jellies
**Range:** Found widely throughout the state; common in the Cascades; often used as an ornamental
**Similarity to toxic species:** None
**Best time:** Summer
**Status:** Common
**Tools needed:** Berry-collecting basket

## PROPERTIES

This is a low-growing to medium-size shrub, though some are low-growing and spreading. Leaves are alternately arranged and pinnately compound. The leaflets are holly-like, with spines along their margins. Flowers are yellow and are formed in racemes. The sepals and petals are similar, usually in five whorls. The approximately ¼-inch fruits are bluish to purple berries and are tightly arranged in clusters that resemble tiny grapes.

Though Oregon grape can be found throughout the state, it is most common in the west, in wooded areas. It is also planted as an ornamental, so it will be found outside its native terrain.

Fruits of the Oregon grape

## USES

My experience with the Oregon grape is mostly as a trail nibble, and on occasion I have mashed at least a handful to use as a pancake topping. These small oval berries are tart and refreshing, high in vitamin C, and make a good jelly when lightly sweetened with honey.

According to Cecilia Garcia and Dr. James Adams in *Healing with Medicinal Plants of the West*, the fruits of all the members of the *Berberis* genus, generally all commonly called "Oregon grape," were eaten raw or cooked by most Indians wherever the plant grew. *B. nervosa*'s blue to purplish fruits were gathered by the Yana people from the foothills and dried, then ground into a flour that was used for a mush. Many of the indigenous peoples made drinks from these fruits. They are also quite good dried and used as a snack food or added to cookies, cakes, or other dishes as you'd add raisins.

Oregon grape fruit cluster. Note the leaf shape.

Garcia and Adams noted that the fruit also has antihistamine activity, which may relieve indigestion. And according to Paul Campbell, author of *Earth Pigments and Paint of the California Indians*, the fruits are especially useful in making traditional blue pigment and paint.

# BIRCH FAMILY (Betulaceae)

The Birch family consists of 6 genera and about 155 species worldwide. Three of these genera are found in Washington.

Leaf and double-fruit of the hazelnut KEIR MORSE

## HAZELNUT, aka BEAKED HAZELNUT
### Corylus cornuta

The *Corylus* genus has about fifteen species worldwide, with only *C. cornuta* found in Washington. *C. cornuta* is found from British Columbia to California, east to Newfoundland and Georgia; but it is separated into two varieties. The California hazelnut, *C. cornuta* var. *californica*, is found from British Columbia to California, mostly on the west side of the Cascades. The beaked hazelnut, *C. cornuta* var. *cornuta* is a found from British Columbia and the northeastern corner of Washington State to the eastern shores of North America. The two varieties will hybridize where their ranges overlap in southern British Columbia and eastern Oregon.

**Use:** Edible nuts

**Range:** Found on the edges of forests, slopes, and many other habitats throughout. In Washington, prefers shady environments.

**Similarity to toxic species:** None

**Best time:** Late summer into fall, when nuts mature

**Status:** Common

**Tools needed:** Bag or box for collecting

## PROPERTIES

This large shrub or small tree can grow up to 25 feet tall and can easily be mistaken for an alder. The leaves are oval to round, alternate, with a rounded base and pointed tip. The whole leaf is about 3 inches long, with double-toothed margins. The leaves are more or less hairy (really, more like a fine fuzz) on both sides.

The nuts, which mature from September through October, are formed in pairs. A papery, bristly outer husk covers the nut, which has a thin, brittle inner shell. When you see the exposed nut, it will remind you of a commercial filbert, to which it's related. It's relatively easy to identify this tree when you find it, and easy to harvest the nuts.

## USES

This is an excellent nut, and you'd use it in any of the ways in which you'd use a filbert: raw, roasted, slivered, etc. This means you can shell them and eat them raw in nut mixes, in salads, and even sprinkled into bread or pancake batter. Try sprinkling them on ice cream. The nuts can also be ground into a meal and used to form cakes or added to other pastry dough.

The hazelnuts

Nuts are one of the great survival foods, since they have the oils necessary for life. They store a long time, provide some quick energy with no cooking, and give our bodies a lot of what they need.

# BORAGE, aka WATERLEAF FAMILY (Boraginaceae)

The Borage family consists of 120 genera and about 2,300 species worldwide. At least twenty-two of these genera are found in Washington.

Mountain bluebells in flower. Note the hanging clusters of flowers. JEAN PAWEK

## MOUNTAIN BLUEBELLS
*Mertensia ciliata*
There are about fifty species worldwide, with at least seven in Washington.

**Use:** Edible
**Range:** Generally found in the mountains, along stream banks
**Similarity to toxic species:** None
**Best time:** Spring
**Status:** Somewhat common within its range
**Tools needed:** Container for collecting

## PROPERTIES
This plant will grow in the dry sagebrush country of eastern Washington, though generally it is a mountain plant, found along streams and in meadows. Its most common range is from the foothills to the subalpine.

Mountain bluebells, also known as streamside bluebells, begin with many stems at a woody base, growing up to 4 feet tall with large clusters of stems and many flowers. The basal leaves are elliptical in shape, with a long petiole. The leaves that develop on the stems are smaller, still elliptical, and are nearly stemless (sessile).

The blue flowers are formed in branched, hanging clusters, with petals approximately ½ inch long, and nearly united so that the flowers appear tubular. The styles (the stalklike part of the pistil) extend slightly beyond the petals. The overall appearance is of hanging bells, hence the name.

In general, all species of *Mertensia* can be used for food, and all are generally called bluebells. Sometimes these are referred to as "chiming bells" to differentiate them from the many other unrelated plants that are often also called "bluebells." There are perhaps seven to nine species of *Mertensia* in this area. The tall species that grow 1–4 feet tall and found in moist habitats are *M. ciliata* and *M. paniculata*. Shorter species, smaller than 1 foot, are found at the higher and drier subalpine to alpine areas. These include *M. oblongifolia*, *M. longiflora*, *M. bella*, and *M. perplexa*.

Mountain bluebell flowers
ROBER STEERS

Another view of the flowers JOHN DOYEN

## USES
The tender leaves can be used as a hiking snack. They have a slight oyster-like flavor.

In its zone, this is one of the best green plants you can find. The leaves, tender stems, and flowers can all be used raw for salad when the entire plant is still succulent, or you can just trim off the young tips and stir-fry, steam, or sauté them. You could even add some fresh leaves to a sandwich.

Older plants can get a little hairy, though this doesn't detract from palatability. Still, older leaves are best cooked.

## CAUTIONS
This plant is considered toxic if you consume it in "large" quantities, due to the presence of various alkaloids. We've not heard of any recorded cases of toxicity, however.

# MUSTARD FAMILY (Brassicaceae)

The Mustard family is another large family, comprising more than 330 genera world-wide and about 3,780 species. This large family is subdivided into eight groups. In Washington, the Mustard family is represented by at least fifty-six genera.

The floral characteristics that define the Mustard family are four free petals, four sepals (generally white or yellow, but other colors as well), six stamens (four long, two short), one pistil, a superior ovary, and fruits generally a capsule or silique with two valves. Many are cultivated for foods and some for ornamentals. Botanists divide this family into eight groups. Dr. Leonid Enari stated that he was unaware of any toxic member of this entire family, though some are more palatable than others. As a result, I have experimented with many of the Mustard family species in various parts of North America. The most obvious edible members are presented here.

The typical leaf shape for this family is lyrately pinnate, meaning a large terminal lobe and smaller lateral lobes. Once I asked a fellow botanist for help in identifying the genus of a plant I'd found, which I knew was in the Mustard family. He replied, "Trying to identify a Brassicaceae when not in flower is not exactly fun." Well said! These are much easier to identify once they have flowered.

## WINTERCRESS
*Barbarea vulgaris* and *B. verna*

Wintercress rosette

There are approximately twenty-two species of *Barbarea* worldwide, and three are found in Washington.

**Use:** Leaves are eaten.
**Range:** Common in disturbed soils, fields, and along roads
**Similarity to toxic species:** None
**Best time:** Spring
**Status:** Found widely throughout the state, common in areas
**Tools needed:** Collecting bag

## PROPERTIES

When you see wintercress for the first time, you will notice the obvious resemblance to watercress. Of course they are both in the Mustard family, and both have the same lyrately pinnate leaves so typical of many member of this family.

Wintercress leaves have the same shade of green you see in watercress. However, watercress is found only in the water or at the edges of slow-moving streams. Wintercress is found anywhere, and usually *not* in the water. It grows in the soil, usually disturbed soil. It can be near the water, but it can also be far from water. However, it would not be uncommon to find wintercress in a roadside ditch where water collects.

Wintercress leaves, typical of the Mustard family

It's called wintercress because it has the ability to live through the winter, to overwinter, when most other plants die from the frost.

The leaves tend to form a rosette, and the plant doesn't sprawl like watercress. One of the key differences is that watercress has white flowers and wintercress has yellow flowers. The flower structure of wintercress is like that of all members of this family: four petals, four sepals, six stamens (two short, four tall), and one pistil.

Wintercress flower BARBARA KOLANDER

## USES

Taste a bit of the wintercress. You'll find it a bit bitter, even when young. The leaf is not strongly bitter, but it's bitter nevertheless. For this reason, you'll probably not use these leaves as an exclusive salad ingredient. They can be mixed with other ingredients for a salad, with an oil dressing to help mellow the bitterness. Of course everyone is different, and if you like this flavor, by all means, enjoy it abundantly in your salads.

Wintercress is better as a cooked green, either boiled or steamed, in soups, stews, egg dishes, etc. The tender tops of the plants (leaves and immature flowers) can be boiled or steamed and served with butter, cheese, or other cooked vegetables.

As with every wild food, I always recommend trying this by itself so you get to know the plant's characteristics. Then you'll probably see why the plant is usually cooked and typically blended with other foods to offset the bitterness.

According to the Live Gourmet company, which hydroponically grows *Barbarea verna*, with roots attached, for sale in supermarkets under the trade name of "upland cress," *B. verna* is "high in phytonutrients, antioxidants and vitamins . . . with as much vitamin C as an orange, more calcium than milk, high levels of magnesium, lutein, phosphorus, potassium, iron, beta-carotene, vitamins A, B1, B6, K, rich in fiber and zero fat."

The typical mustard leaf shape

## MUSTARD
*Brassica* spp.
There are thirty-five species worldwide, and at least five are found in Washington.

**Use:** Leaves raw or cooked, seeds for spice, flowers for garnish
**Range:** Fields, urban areas, and dry hillsides
**Similarity to toxic species:** None
**Best time:** Spring for greens and flowers
**Status:** Widespread
**Tools needed:** None

## PROPERTIES
Though you should learn to recognize the common mustards even when the plant is not in flower, it is the flower that will initially draw you to the plant. The yellow flower has the typical Mustard family flora arrangement: four petals (shaped in an X or cross), four sepals (one under each

FORAGER NOTE: This is a hardy plant. I have managed to find some mustard greens even during droughts when no other greens were available.

petal), six stamens (four long, two short), and one pistil. These are formed in a raceme with the buds toward the tops, then the mature flowers, and then, lower on the stalk, the seedpods forming. The seedpods are about 1 inch long and needle thin.

The initial basal leaves are lyrately pinnately divided, meaning they have the appearance of a guitar with a large round lateral lobe and smaller side lobes. Not exactly like a guitar, but that gives you a good mental picture. As the plant matures, the leaves that form on the upper stalks are smaller and linear and look nothing like the young basal leaves.

Mustard plant beginning to flower

## USES

Mustard is one of the first wild foods I began to eat, partly because it is so common, and partly because it is so easy to identify. I recall seeing a line drawing of it in Bradford Angier's book *Free*

Mustard flowers

Forager Barbara Kolander collecting mustard flowers

*for the Eating*, which didn't look anything like the green plant with yellow flowers that I was seeing everywhere. Angier used a picture of the mature plant gone to seed, and I was seeing the young spring plant. They were both right, but it demonstrated the need to always learn plants by observing them in the field.

I began with the young mustard greens, chewing the raw leaves and enjoying the spicy flavor, despite the fine hairs covering the leaves (not all *Brassica* species are hairy). I then moved on to chopping them up and adding to salads, which was good. I next began to boil the leaves and serve them to my family with butter. Everyone enjoyed them, even my father. Eventually I found that I could add mustard

The author with a particularly large black mustard plant
HELEN NYERGES

A rosette of the young black mustard

greens to just about any dish: soups, mixed salads, omelets, stir-fries, potatoes, you name it!

The flower buds and flowers have also been a good trail treat, and they make a colorful garnish to salads and soups. I give them to children and tell them that they taste like broccoli; most of the children say they enjoy the flowers.

The tender tops of the stems with the flower buds can also be snapped off the upper part of the plant, steamed, and served with some sauce or cheese. The flavor is just like the Chinese broccoli you buy at farmers' markets.

You can come back to this annual plant in late fall, when the leaves are dried up and the tops are just tan-colored stems with small seedpods. Collect the pods in a bag, and break them up. The seeds go to the bottom of the bag, and you can discard the pod shells. The brown seeds are then used as a seasoning for various dishes calling for mustard, or you can try making your own mustard from them.

## RECIPE

### Pascal's Mustard

Fellow forager Pascal Baudar takes the pungent flowers of the regular black mustard and grinds them while fresh, adding white wine and vinegar to taste. He thus produces a mustard condiment from the flowers, not from the seeds as is the usual custom. This makes a delicious mustard with a new twist.

Young sea rocket plant, growing in the sand RICK ADAMS

## SEA ROCKET
*Cakile edentula* and *C. maritima*

There are seven species of *Cakile* world-wide, and two are found in Washington. Sea rocket is found on the beach shores of North America, Africa, and Europe. On Washington's west coast, we have *C. edentula* (American sea rocket) and *C. maritima* (European sea rocket), both introduced.

**Use:** Greens, sprouts, and flowers are edible, ideally cooked, but can be used raw sparingly.
**Range:** Restricted to the sandy beaches along the entire coast
**Similarity to toxic species:** None
**Best time:** Spring, but can be picked year-round
**Status:** Somewhat common
**Tools needed:** None

Flowers of the sea rocket RICK ADAMS

## PROPERTIES

Sea rocket is widespread along the Washington coast, growing in the sand, in the upper areas of the beach, usually just beyond the high-tide line in the dunes. When you see how well these plants have naturalized, it is hard to believe they are not natives. *C. maritima* is the one that you see most commonly on the beaches, and it is native to Europe. *C. edentula* is also found and is native to the East Coast of the United States.

The leaves are very much like a small mustard leaf, but plump, as if the mustard leaf was swollen. Each leaf has a bluish-green appearance, with the leaves pinnately divided into linear segments. Typically, each leaf tends to fold inward along its central vein. The seedpods also look swollen, and you can see why the plant is called "rocket" by looking at the pod's space-rocket appearance.

The "plump" seed capsules of sea rocket
RICK ADAMS

The normal habitat of sea rocket, in the sand above the high-tide line RICK ADAMS

Sea rocket plant in flower RICK ADAMS

Of course the lavender to light purple flower has the typical mustard flower arrangement of four petals, four sepals, six stamens, and one pistil.

## USES

The leaves are strongly flavored like horseradish, and generally you would not want to include the mature leaves in a salad. But boiling tones them down quite a bit, and they are then tastier and more palatable. The boiled leaves can be added to flavor soup broths or to dishes of mixed greens. In general, you'd probably not want to serve them alone as a cooked green unless you changed the water once and then served them with some onions and probably a savory sauce.

Still, they can turn an otherwise bland meal into quite a treat. They will help flavor clam chowder and other soups and stews, and will really liven up stale old MREs (meals ready to eat).

If you're at the beach during late winter, you might find an old sea rocket plant whose seeds have all dropped into the sand and sprouted. You can carefully harvest dozens of these strongly flavored sprouts and add them to your soup or salad.

Think of sea rocket more as a flavoring agent and garnish, not as a principal food.

## RECIPE

**Ocean Side Wasabi**

Finely dice sea rocket leaves into nearly a paste, then add a very small amount of oil and vinegar to create a passable "wasabi."

A typical array of young shepherd's purse plants

## SHEPHERD'S PURSE
*Capsella bursa-pastoris*
There are four species of *Capsella* worldwide; only this one is found in Washington.

**Use:** Leaves eaten raw or cooked; medicine
**Range:** Prefers lawns, fields, and disturbed soils
**Similarity to toxic species:** None
**Best time:** Spring is best for greens; the seeds can be collected late spring to early summer.
**Status:** Somewhat common
**Tools needed:** None

## PROPERTIES
Shepherd's purse is most easily identified by its flat, heart-shaped seedpods. They are unmistakable! The stalks rise about a foot or so tall. The little clusters of white

Note the heart-shaped seed capsules of the shepherd's purse plant. (In this case, it is rising out of a patch of chickweed.)

flowers, sometimes tinged with a bit of purple, are formed in racemes along the stalk. These then mature into the heart-shaped pods. Trouble is, by the time you see all the seedpods, it's usually too late to use the young leaves for food, but now you know how to recognize shepherd's purse for the next season.

The young leaves are often hidden in the grass, making them somewhat inconspicuous. The basal leaves are toothed, with a large terminal lobe, typical of Mustard family leaves. The upper leaves are without a stalk and are more arrowhead shaped. If you look closely, you'll see that the young leaves are covered with little hairs.

## USES

The flavor of shepherd's purse leaves is mild, and they could be used in just about any recipe, such as salads, sandwiches, soups, eggs, etc. However, they seem to be best when used in salads. Some Native Americans ground the seeds into a meal and used it in drinks and as a flour for various dishes.

Dr. Leonid Enari used to poll his students on which plant tasted the best of the many wild plants he let them try. Consistently in his polls, shepherd's purse was rated the best. It is actually somewhat bland and peppery, but not *too* peppery, and the texture is mild. Even finicky eaters will like these leaves.

It's also very nutritious. About ½ cup of the leaves (100 g) contains 208 mg of calcium, 86 mg of phosphorus, 40 mg of sodium, 394 mg of potassium, 36 mg of vitamin C, and 1,554 IU (international units) of vitamin A.

Dr. Enari told his students that this was the best plant to stop nosebleed. You boil the plant, dip a cotton ball into the water, and then apply to the nose. It turns out that many people have used this plant medicinally, especially to stop internal or external bleeding.

Flowering bittercress plant

## BITTERCRESS
*Cardamine* spp.

There are about 200 species of *Cardamine* worldwide, and 14 can be found in Washington, all edible. The most common seem to be *C. hirsuta* and *C. oligosperma*.

**Use:** Leaves and all tender portions can be eaten.

**Range:** Common in the western United States, including parts of Washington. Likes disturbed soils; especially common in gardens and nurseries.

**Similarity to toxic species:** None

**Best time:** Spring

**Status:** Widespread in localized areas

**Tools needed:** None

Bittercress in hand, to see the human scale

## PROPERTIES

Bittercress can be very common in certain areas, mostly in gardens, where it appears as a common weed. The plant prefers moist and disturbed soils. It grows from sea level up to the foothills.

The small plant begins with a somewhat orderly appearing rosette of pinnately divided basal leaves. Each leaflet is generally round, all about the same size, though the terminal lobe is slightly larger—which is the case in just about all members of the Mustard family, except these leaves are very small. Each leaf can be about 2 inches long, with the terminal lobe about ½ inch wide.

One or more flower stalks may arise from the root. As the flower stalk arises, the leaves appearing on the stalk are similar, though the leaflets become more linear.

The bright white flowers appear mostly in the early spring and the early fall, though you can find the plant in flower nearly year-round. The flower pattern, like all members of the Mustard family, is four petals, four sepals, six stamens, and one pistil. The seedpods that follow the flowers are thin, like little needles, and about 1 inch long.

Though somewhat short-lived, the plant can be collected anytime in its growing season. The little seedpods of this plant are known to pop open, throwing the seeds, which is why the plant can be found so abundantly within local areas.

## USES

If you have a garden, you've probably pulled *C. oligosperma* or *C. hirsute* out of your pots and garden space, whether you knew its name or not. It's a small plant, it's an annual, and it spreads—and spreads. Gardeners seem to hate it, even though they could eat it. Most gardeners and nurserymen I've talked to regard this as a serious nuisance plant, along with oxalis. At least one person questioned why I would even consider including a plant such as this in a book of edible wild plants. "Because it's edible!" I replied.

The leaves are good raw when very young and can be added to salads, soups, and various cooked dishes. They become just a bit stronger and bitter as they mature. In fact, any tender part of the

Bittercress growing in a potted plant

plant can be added to a salad, soup, stew, or other cooked dish. The older leaves are edible too. They can have a stronger flavor, but cooking mellows them and makes them more palatable.

You would not make a whole meal from this plant, partly because the leaves are so tiny that it takes a bit of time to gather a reasonable amount, and then it cooks down to very little bulk. But if you have this plant in abundance, you shouldn't overlook it. It's a nutritious, tasty addition to many dishes, as well as sandwiches. Consider it more of a garnish or spice when you add it your meals. When in season and abundant, it's easy to collect several handfuls. Rinse them to get rid of dirt, and add to your salad for a spicy addition.

I also find bittercress tasty when cooked like spinach, though it is a bit of work to collect enough for one pot of greens.

Watercress in the stream

## WATERCRESS
*Nasturtium officinale*
There are five species of *Nasturtium* worldwide, with at least two found in Washington.

**Use:** Leaves eaten raw or cooked in salads, stir-fries, soups, etc.; can be dried for use as seasoning
**Range:** Restricted to the edges of lakes and streams
**Similarity to toxic species:** None
**Best time:** Summer, before the plant flowers; however, the plant can be collected anytime.
**Status:** Somewhat common along streams
**Tools needed:** None

### PROPERTIES
Once you learn to recognize watercress and see how the pinnately divided leaves are formed, you will find it quite easy to recognize, whether it is very young or older and flowering. First, it nearly always grows directly on the edges of streams where the water is slower. Occasionally you'll find it in sandy areas, but it is always an area that is at least seasonally underwater. You'll typically find it growing in thick mats.

The leaves are pinnately divided into round leaflets. The stems are hollow, and there are white hairs on the underwater part of the stem. The plant is in the Mustard family, so when it gets older and flowers, the white flowers will be divided into the typical Mustard formula: four petals, four sepals, six stamens, and one pistil.

Though watercress can be found worldwide today, it is regarded by botanists as a native plant. It was known to be a part of the diet of early Native Americans.

## USES

Watercress was one of the very first wild plants that I learned to identify and began to use. It is not only common throughout waterways in Washington, but throughout the world.

I have always enjoyed making a salad of mixed greens, including watercress. But I don't usually make a salad with *only* watercress because it's a bit too spicy for my taste. A few raw watercress leaves are also tasty in sandwiches.

Watercress makes a delicious soup. Just finely chop the entire plant (tender stems and leaves) and add it

The author collecting fresh watercress along the bank of a stream BARBARA KOLANDER

to a water- or milk-based soup. Or you can add chopped watercress leaves to a miso base.

You can also cook the greens like spinach, serving with a simple seasoning such as butter or cheese. Or try mixing the greens into an egg omelet. If you're living off MREs or freeze-dried camping food, you can add some diced watercress to liven up your meals.

Also, for those of you who like making your own spices, you can dry and powder watercress and use it to season various dishes. Use it alone, or blend the powdered watercress with powdered seaweed or other flavorful herbs. You'll notice that some of the commercial salt-alternative spices use dried watercress leaves.

Another self-reliance idea is to dry wild foods into the basis of a soup stock and then reconstitute later into a soup or stew broth. Dried and powdered watercress makes an ideal ingredient in such a mix.

Watercress has numerous medicinal applications. Some of the most popular, and most documented, include eating watercress to prevent eczema from returning or for inflammatory flare-ups, as well as using an extract of watercress (obtained by boiling the leaves for ten minutes in water) as a disinfectant to wash the eczema area.

As a tea, watercress acts as a digestive aid; the mustard oil glycosides, vitamins, and bitters in the tea promote production of the stomach juices that aid digestion. With its high potassium content, watercress tea assists the kidneys by acting as a diuretic, cleansing the urinary tract. Because watercress contains high levels of lutein, an essential antioxidant for eye health, eating it is good for your eyes. Consuming watercress, or drinking a tea from the leaves, is also helpful with respiratory problems, due to its expectorant qualities and magnesium content.

In fact, you get all these benefits, more or less, by consuming any member of the Mustard family, though watercress and wintercress have been studied the most (source for medicinal aspects: www.LiveGourmet.com).

Watercress leaves

## CAUTIONS

If you have doubts about the purity of the water where you get your watercress, you should not eat it raw; boil it first and then use it in a cooked dish. Always wash watercress before using it. It grows right in the water, and you want to remove any dirt or other undesirables that may be clinging to the plant.

RECIPE

**Saturday Night Special**

Gently sauté ½ onion bulb, diced, in a skillet with butter. You could substitute a handful of wild or garden onion greens. Quickly add at least 1 cup watercress, chopped into large pieces, and cook gently until all is tender. Add a dash of soy sauce and serve.

Wild radish plant

# WILD RADISH
*Raphanus sativus* and *R. raphanistrum*

There are three species of *Raphanus* worldwide. These two, both native to the Mediterranean, are found in Washington. The latter is also referred to as "jointed charlock."

**Use:** All tender portions of this plant—leaves, stems, pods, flowers—can be eaten raw, pickled, or cooked. Roots generally are not used.

**Range:** Fields, wet areas, farmlands, vacant lots, and disturbed soils

**Similarity to toxic species:** None

**Best time:** Spring into summer

**Status:** Common

**Tools needed:** Clippers

The four-petaled wild radish flower

Wild radish leaf

## PROPERTIES

Each young leaf of the wild radish is lyrately pinnately divided, meaning there is one large end lobe and smaller side lobes or segments to the leaf. It resembles a guitar! When the young leaves of wild radish are newly emerging, it would be easy to confuse the leaves with those of mustard (*Brassica* spp.). However, wild radish leaves lack the fine hairs that you find on mustard. If you examine a wild radish leaf closely, you'll see that it's covered somewhat sparsely with bristles, but the leaf is smoother (than mustard) and you will see a tinge of red in the midrib of the radish leaf.

As the plant flowers, instead of the usual yellow mustard flowers, the flowers will be lavender or white or, very rarely, a pale yellow. There is the typical Mustard family flower formula of four petals, four sepals, six stamens (four long and two short), and one pistil. The flowers are followed by fleshy seedpods that resemble pointed jalapeño peppers.

The root of wild radish is a white taproot, not at all like the radish you might grow in your garden or buy at the store. It is largely woody and inedible, though there is a soft outer layer that can be peeled off. The taste of this outer root layer is so obviously "radish" that most anyone can identify this plant by that aroma and flavor.

Wild radish can grow up to 4 feet, even taller in ideal conditions.

Succulent pods of the wild radish. Pods are great as is or pickled, as long as you pickle them before they mature and harden.

## USES

The wild radish has many edible parts. The leaves can be collected at any time in their growing cycle, cut into small pieces, and added to salads. They are hot and spicy, so add to other greens. The leaves can also be added to soups, stews, and egg dishes.

The flowers are quite tasty and sweet when you first pick and nibble them, but your mouth will get very hot. Eat them sparingly. You can pick the flowers and add them to salads and other dishes as a tasty garnish. The tender flower tips—somewhat resembling Chinese broccoli—can be snapped free, steamed or boiled, and served with butter, cheese, or a spicy sauce.

Explorer Ben Hererra examines the root of a wild radish. In general, only the soft outer skin is used; the interior of the root is too woody.

The green seedpods, which somewhat resemble jalapeño or serrano chilies, can be nibbled when they are still tender inside and haven't gotten woody. You can add the chopped tender pods to soups and salads, or try pickling them.

When we think of a radish, we automatically think of a red fleshy root, usually served as a garnish. However, the wild radish is a white carrot-like taproot that is generally too tough to eat. Usually, there is enough of a skin layer on the root that you can peel it, wash it, and add that spicy outer layer to soups or salads.

Occasionally, if the conditions of soil and moisture are right, you may find a tender root that can be entirely eaten. They are best when sliced thin and added to salads, stews, soups, and other mixtures.

# PINK FAMILY (Caryophyllaceae)

The Pink family consists of 83 to 89 genera (depending on which authority) and about 3,000 species worldwide. At least twenty-eight genera are found in Washington.

Chickweed

## CHICKWEED
### Stellaria media

There are 190 species of *Stellaria* worldwide, with at least 14 found in Washington.

**Use:** The leaves are best raw in salads, but can also be cooked in various dishes or dried and powdered to make into pasta.

**Range:** Moist and shady areas in urban settings, mountain canyons, and along rivers. Scattered widely where the conditions are ideal.

**Similarity to toxic species:** You may find young common spurge (*Euphorbia peplus*) in chickweed patches. It superficially resembles chickweed, but spurge doesn't have the line of white hairs, its stalk is more erect, and the leaves are alternate, not opposite like chickweed. If you break the stem of spurge, you will see a white sap; it shouldn't be eaten.

**Best time:** Spring; chickweed rarely lasts beyond midsummer.

**Status:** Common

**Tools needed:** None

## PROPERTIES

Chickweed is one of the introduced *Stellaria* species that is now widespread in Washington. In fact, today it can be found worldwide. It is common in urban yards, shady fields, and canyons. It is a short-lived annual that shrivels up by summer when the soil is dry.

Chickweed is a low-growing, sprawling annual that first arises after the winter rains. The thin stem will grow up to 1 foot long, and upon close inspection, you'll see a line of fine white hairs along one side of the stem. The oval-shaped leaves, arranged in pairs along the stem, come to a sharp tip. The flowers are white and five-petaled, though it may appear to have ten petals because each petal has a deep cleft.

Chickweed has a tender stem, opposite leaves, and small five-petaled white flowers.

## USES

Chickweed is probably best used as a salad ingredient. In a thick patch of chickweed, one can cut off a handful of the stems just above the root. Then you just rinse the leaves, dice, and add salad dressing.

The plant can also be cooked in soups and stews. For those who are more adventurous, the entire chickweed plant (above-ground) can be dried, powdered, and mixed 50/50 with wheat flour, then run through a pasta machine. The result is a green pasta with a flavor of chickweed.

A closer look at the young chickweed plant

Fresh-picked chickweed, rinsed and ready to make salad

FORAGER NOTE: Back in the 1970s, one of the people I went mushroom hunting with was Florence Nishida, one of the best mycologists I have known. Listen to what Florence recently told me:

"Did I tell you I loathe chickweed? It's been a constant weeding task for me in my home garden (we've kept it out of our teaching garden). The reason probably (because the smell is unpleasant to me) is that when we Japanese were in the [Manzanar internment] camp, especially in the first months, but even later, the army provided meals that were pretty bad. My mother tried to supplement by picking chickweed, which grew wild around the camp, to feed me. I wasn't fond of it, probably because she kept pushing it. The nose-to-brain connection is pretty strong."

Florence is referring to the Japanese internment camps of the World War II era. She added that the Japanese actually made adobe bricks and built the camp gymnasium by hand (though it is all gone today). She added, "You can see evidence of the work the Japanese did to bring agriculture to the camp. They enabled the growing of food in that very, very desolate Mohave Desert, a low desert with very little vegetation. They taught the Indians (whose reservation was used by the US government to build the camp on) how to irrigate and grow food."

## RECIPE

### Mia's Chickweed Soup

Although chickweed can be found on city sidewalks, it's best to gather it in the wild, away from pesticides. As an homage to their humble origins, I call this my "Sidewalk Soup." It's simple, low fat (you can omit the pancetta or bacon and it's still amazing), and has a surprising depth of flavor reminiscent of spring peas and pea shoots. This is my version of "wild split-pea soup."

4–5 tablespoons diced pancetta (or bacon)
1 medium onion, diced
1 stalk celery, diced
1 carrot, diced
1 teaspoon olive oil, as needed
4–5 cloves garlic, finely minced
1 teaspoon fennel seeds
1 small Oregon myrtle leaf
1 small white sage leaf
2 teaspoons French or Italian herbs (I like oregano, thyme, and parsley)
1 small potato, cubed
6 cups packed chickweed, washed and chopped
1 teaspoon raw apple cider vinegar (to keep mixture green)
Salt and pepper to taste

In a heated stockpot, sauté the pancetta or bacon until crisp. Add onion, celery, and carrots and sauté until translucent. You may need to add a bit of olive oil to the bottom of the pan, approximately 1 teaspoon. Add the garlic and spices and continue to sauté until just fragrant. Add the cubed potato; it will serve to thicken the soup, once pureed. Add the chickweed (save a handful for garnish) and enough water to cover the chickweed with an inch of water. Cover and bring to a boil. Add the vinegar, then reduce to a light simmer for about 20–30 minutes.

Once slightly cooled, transfer to a food processor and puree the mixture. Add salt and pepper to taste. Serve with tender, crisp chickweed as garnish. Delish!

—Recipe from Mia Wasilevich

The author teaching students how to identify chickweed RICK ADAMS

Because chickweed grows close to the ground with its fine stems, it is common to find other plants growing in chickweed patches. So you need to make certain you are only collecting chickweed. We've seen poison hemlock growing within chickweed patches.

# GOOSEFOOT FAMILY (Chenopodiaceae)

The Goosefoot family consists of 100 genera and about 1,500 species worldwide, found especially in the deserts and saline or alkaline soils. Some are cultivated for food. There are thirteen genera in Washington. (Some botanists have lumped this family into Amaranthaceae.)

According to Dr. Leonid Enari, this is one of those very promising plant families for food. His research indicated that most of the leaves could be used for food, either raw or cooked, if too bitter and unpalatable. Dr. Enari also stated that the majority of the seeds could be harvested, winnowed, and ground and used as a flour or flour extender.

## LAMB'S QUARTER, WHITE AND GREEN
### *Chenopodium album* and *C. murale*
There are about one hundred species of *Chenopodium* worldwide, with about nineteen species found in Washington.

Young white lamb's quarter

Another view of white lamb's quarter

**Use:** Leaves eaten raw or cooked; seeds added to soups or bread batter; leaves dried for seasoning
**Range:** Prefers disturbed soils of farms, gardens, hillsides, fields, along trails, etc.
**Similarity to toxic species:** Black nightshade leaves can be mistaken for lamb's quarter leaves when very young. Be sure to look for the white mealy (and "sparkly") underside of lamb's quarter, and for the streak of red in the axils.
**Best time:** Spring for the leaves; late summer for the seeds
**Status:** Common and widespread
**Tools needed:** None

FORAGER NOTE: Everyone should get to know lamb's quarter. Not only is it widespread in Washington, but it can also be found throughout the world. I once spent a week in the mountains, eating only lamb's quarter (salad, soup, fried, boiled). It is a plant that I can depend on finding even during a drought when nothing else is available.

A patch of white lamb's quarter that has gone to seed

## PROPERTIES

Lamb's quarter is a plant that everyone has seen, but probably not recognized. It's an annual plant that sprouts up in the spring and summer in fields, gardens, and disturbed soils, and generally grows about 3–4 feet tall. (I did record one at 12 feet, but that's the exception.)

The leaf shape is roughly triangular, somewhat resembling a goose's or duck's foot, hence the family name. The color of the stem and leaves is light green, and the axils of the leaves, and sometimes the stem, are streaked with red. The bottom of each leaf is covered with a mealy substance, causing raindrops to bead up on the leaf.

Explorer Ben Hererra prepares to gather some leaves of white lamb's quarter for lunch.

A young green lamb's quarter. Note the "shinier" glossy leaf.

Another green lamb's quarter plant. Note the red veins in the stem

As the plant matures over the season, the inconspicuous green flowers will appear; seeds will form as the plant dries and withers.

## USES

Lamb's quarter is a versatile plant that can be used in many recipes. The young tender leaves can be cut into smaller pieces and used in a salad. The leaves and tender stems can be cooked like spinach and seasoned for a tasty dish. The water from this cooking makes a delicious broth. The leaves are a versatile green, which I've used as an addition to soups, egg dishes, and quiche, and even stir-fried with other vegetables.

Lamb's quarter will go to seed by late summer, and seeds from the dead plant are harvestable for several months. The seed is an excellent source of calcium, phosphorus, and potassium, according to the USDA. Collect the seeds by hand and place in a large salad bowl, then rub them between your hands to remove the chaff. Next, winnow them by letting handfuls drop into the salad bowl as

A dish being prepared by sautéing lamb's quarter greens and tomatoes

you gently blow off the chaff. The seeds can then be added to soups, rice dishes, and bread batter.

## CAUTIONS

Older leaves may cause slight irritation to the throat when eaten raw, without dressing. Trevor Wire from Leavenworth, Washington, shares the following experience:

"I ate the raw tender tops of lamb's quarters two days in a row and, about two hours later, each time, found myself in the bathroom with the slightest case of diarrhea. No big deal. I looked it up and learned about the presence of oxalic acid in the *raw*, which can have this effect. Supposedly it can be cooked out with boiling or steaming. I tried that, and it tastes better and doesn't bother my stomach. Also, I know that the plants I was eating were too old for raw consumption, because they were definitely bitter."

Young glasswort growing in the sand

## GLASSWORT, aka PICKLEWEED
*Salicornia* spp.
There are about fifty species of *Salicornia* worldwide, but only *S. rubra* and *S. depressa* are believed to grow in Washington.

**Use:** The tender stems can be eaten raw, cooked, or pickled.
**Range:** Found along the Pacific coast above high tide, along the rivers that feed into the ocean, and in the back-bay areas
**Similarity to toxic species:** None
**Best time:** Spring
**Status:** Common locally
**Tools needed:** Clippers

### PROPERTIES
Glasswort is typically found in the back bays and sand flats above the high-tide areas of the Pacific Ocean. I have seen acres of nearly just glasswort in such places. But it will also grow somewhat solitary, and in some of the fields and wild areas not too far from the beaches.

Another view of glasswort growing at the beach

The plant stems—about ¼ inch thick—have the appearance of swollen fingers, sort of, but not so thick, with distinct joints. The stalks are a pale green color—almost translucent—and then turn red in the fall. The entire plant rises no more than a few inches high. There are no apparent leaves. There are flowers and seeds, but these are usually very inconspicuous. The overall appearance of the plant is of small swollen stalks.

## USES
Glasswort makes a great beachside nibble—a little here, a little there. It's also good added to salads, but not too much. Just gently pinch the tender tips and add sparingly to salads, because in volume it may be a bit too strong and overpowering. Plus, you need to gather it young enough, before it gets woody and largely inedible.

Older glasswort stems have begun to turn red.

Cooked, glasswort's flavor is just right when added to soups, chowders, and even omelets. I suggest you taste a little first and experiment before adding a lot to your dishes. In some cases, you might find that the flavor is greatly improved by boiling the tender stems, pouring off the water, and then adding the glasswort to your various cooked dishes.

I have enjoyed a very simple pickled glasswort too. Just collect the tender young sections of the stems, before they get woody on the inside. Pack them loosely in a jar, cover with raw apple cider vinegar, and put the jar in your refrigerator. In about a month they will make a great garnish and side for various dishes. You can also make your glasswort pickles a bit milder by boiling them briefly, rinsing them, and then putting them into the glass jar with vinegar.

# HEATH FAMILY (Ericaceae)

The Heath family contains about 100 genera and 3,000 species worldwide. In Washington, there are twenty-six genera of this family.

## MADRONE
### *Arbutus menziesii*

There are about twenty species of *Arbutus*; madrone is the only native species found in Washington.

**Use:** Edible fruits

**Range:** Most common in the drier, lower elevations in the western side of the Cascades

**Similarity to toxic species:** None

**Best time:** Summer

**Status:** Somewhat common

**Tools needed:** Container to collect fruit

### PROPERTIES

A shrub or tree, with reddish bark that is typically shedding and curling. The leaves are alternate, leathery, and evergreen. Each leaf is oblong to ovate, 4–5 inches long, with small and shallow serrations. The white or pinkish petals are fused into a very characteristic down-hanging urn shape. The distinctive fruit is round, diameter about ¼ inch, and orange-red in color. The fruit is papillate, meaning it is uniformly covered with small roundish bumps.

This is a somewhat common wild bush, or tree, along the Washington coast and in the interior. If you've ever seen the strawberry tree (*Arbutus unedo*), sometimes

Madrone tree RICK ADAMS

Madrone leaf RICK ADAMS

used as a horticultural plant, you will notice the resemblance between it and the madrone.

The madrone leaves are around 4 inches in length, and the leaf margin is entire or minutely serrate. The upper surface of the madrone leaf is bright green, and its bottom side is whitish. Madrone has drooping bell- or lantern-shaped flowers, which consist of five sepals, five petals, ten stamens, and one pistil. Of course, the most conspicuous part of the madrone is the round fruits, about ¼ inch in diameter. They are round, maroon-colored, and covered with bumps. When you cut the fruits in half, you'll see five chambers. The texture is much more substantial than a strawberry. The fruit is on the dry side, mealy, and substantial. However, the sugar content is low.

Bark of the madrone RICK ADAMS

Mature fruit of the madrone JULIE KIERSTEAD NELSON

Immature fruit of the madrone DAN BAIRD

Though the fruit can make a decent nibble, it is definitely improved by soaking in water, and perhaps even cooking it and adding a bit of honey to make a cider.

My mentor, Dr. Enari, used to let his students try the related strawberry tree fruits. He'd say, "Yes, edible, but no flavor."

## USES

The manners in which certain Northern California tribes used madrone fruits are perhaps still the best ways to enjoy them. The Pomo and Bear River Band ate these berries fresh, as well as roasted, parched, and stored for later use.

The Miwok used madrone like manzanita, and made the fruits into a cider. This is done simply by soaking the berries in warm water for a while, straining out the fruit, and then sweetening the water with honey or some other sweetener. The flavor will vary from mildly sweet to almost flavorless, depending on the quality of the fruit you collected, and perhaps how late in the season you collected it.

The Karok dried the fruits and reconstituted them later, and sometimes mixed them with processed manzanita fruit. The Yurok roasted the berries over a fire before eating them, which would be a great way to process them during a camping trip.

### RECIPE

**Madrone Tea**

A good way to enjoy madrone is to make a beverage from the peels of the bark. Margit Roos-Collins, author of *The Flavors of Home*, describes taking about five peelings of the colorful madrone bark (about ¾ inch of the bark), putting it into a cup, and pouring boiling water over it. She describes the flavor as mild, like Chinese green tea with a hint of wood. The tea has a cinnamon color. She suggests trying it in different ways: plain, with honey, with milk, with a cinnamon stick, or mixed with other teas.

The sprawling kinnikinnick plant ALGIE AU

## KINNIKINNICK
*Arctostaphylos uva-ursi*
There are sixty-two species of *Arctostaphylos* worldwide, with at least five species found in Washington.

**Use:** Leaves used as tea or smoked; fruits eaten or made into a cider
**Range:** In Washington, found in coastal bluffs and prairies, dry subalpine meadows, and dry coniferous forest. It is found widely throughout Washington, Alaska south to California and New Mexico, and east to the Atlantic coast.
**Similarity to toxic species:** None
**Best time:** Summer for the fruits
**Status:** Relatively common
**Tools needed:** Basket for collecting

### PROPERTIES
Kinnikinnick is a low-growing shrub, with its stems trailing across the ground, rarely rising more than 6 inches off the ground. The leathery leaves are alternately arranged, dark green, and rounded at the tip. They are about 1 inch long. Flowers are light pink, urn-shaped small clusters near the tips of stems, very typical of this family. The bright red berries are less than ½ inch across.

Another look at the kinnikinnick plant ALGIE AU

## USES

Kinnikinnick berries are edible, often added to other foods. One botanist wrote that the fruit "tastes like lint." Not exactly appealing. In fact, they are dry with a bland, almost sour, flavor. Sometimes you detect a hint of sweetness. I like them.

Various Northwest tribes (and throughout kinnikinnick's range) have used the berries for food, typically added to other fruits, as well as mixtures including eggs and meats. Think of them as a mild sweetening agent, and they are best when mixed with other foods. Moerman's discussion in his book of all the uses of these fruits is rather extensive and includes desserts, drinks, fried dishes, ice cream, berry dishes, sauces, and main courses, all using kinnikinnick berries.

My favorite recipe involves soaking the mashed berries in warm water—not exactly cooking them, but letting them simmer for half an hour or so. Then I strain out the liquid and sweeten it with just a bit of honey. This makes a very tasty trail cider.

The berries are usually not very abundant, but when you can find them, you should be able to cook them into a tasty dish.

Kinnikinnick is most well known as a traditional alternative to tobacco. It was used as a smoke in the old days, typically mixed with other substances such as dogwood or willow bark. Some have ascribed mild narcotic effects to these leaves, and while that may be so, I have simply enjoyed them as a pleasant smoke in my pipe without all the harmful effects of commercial tobacco. Different groups had their own preferred mixes, and I suggest that you simply try your own experiments until you find what you like. By itself, kinnikinnick doesn't have a strong flavor or aroma, so I have tried various mixes, using such other

Kinnikinnick plant in fruit BARRY BRECKLING

substances as willow bark, mint leaves, mullein leaves, mugwort, and sometimes various sages.

The leaves are leathery and become brittle when dried, so you will need to crush them up into smaller pieces before you can put them into your pipe. Sometimes I blend kinnikinnick with various other herbs in my electric coffee grinder to get a homogenous blend.

The leaves are also used as a tea, made by infusion. Daniel Moerman, in his *Native American Ethnobotany*, lists dozens of ways in which indigenous people of the Northwest and elsewhere used the leaves (usually an infusion from the leaves) to heal wounds. He lists many other similar medicinal applications.

***Note:*** *Kinnikinnick* is an Algonquian term that was originally applied to this plant, referring to something that was mixed, in this case a smoking mix. The term refers to any of the plants that were smoked, usually this one, some willow barks and dogwood, and others. The term has sometimes been used to refer to any nontobacco smoking mix.

## LEWIS AND CLARK
Lewis and Clark described seeing kinnikinnick in bloom several times, which they referred to by the name Sackacommis.

Salal in flower MATT BELOW

## SALAL
*Gaultheria shallon*
The *Gaultheria* genus includes about 130 species, with 4 found in Washington.

**Use:** Fruits are eaten.
**Range:** Salal is found in mixed evergreen forests, redwood forests, and northern coastal scrub. You typically won't find it in wetlands. Found generally along the coast, up to the western edge of the Cascades.
**Similarity to toxic species:** None
**Best time:** Summer
**Status:** Relatively common
**Tools needed:** Basket for collecting

## PROPERTIES
Salal is a native shrub, with ovate leaves that are finely veined. The hanging lantern–type flowers make the relationship of the salal plant to the manzanita very clear. The flowers appear in a line along the stalk, and as the berries develop, they are likewise in a line along the stalk. The berries are dark purple to more or less blue-black in color. When mature, the end of the fruit has what appears to be a five-point indented star.

The plant is a low-growing to medium-size evergreen shrub with either spreading or erect stalks. It grows in moist areas, along the margins of forests, in

Salal plant with fruit LILY JANE TSONG

some cases being the most dominant plant. The leaves are alternate, ovate to elliptical, about 3 to 4 inches in length. The leaves are finely toothed, leathery, and conspicuously veined.

## USES
The Pomo, Karok, and other indigenous people are known to have eaten salal berries fresh. These were widely used and were prepared in many different ways. The berries were dried and formed into cakes, which were saved for later. The cakes would sometimes be dipped in oil and cooked, or be reconstituted by boiling and then eaten. The fruits might

Salal fruit ZOYA AKULOVA

also be mixed with other dried berries and stored for winter use. Jam, jellies, and pies were all made from salal.

The Karok also used the fresh fruits as a dye for basket caps. Among other tribes, a switch off the branches was used for making soap from soapberries.

## LEWIS AND CLARK
On December 9 and December 27, 1805, William Clark wrote about the meals his Native hosts prepared for him where salal was a major ingredient.

Huckleberry in fruit ZOYA AKULOVA

## HUCKLEBERRY AND BLUEBERRY
### *Vaccinium* spp.

The *Vaccinium* genus includes more than 400 species worldwide, with at least 13 found in Washington. In general, Vacciniums are often referred to as huckleberries, blueberries, cranberries, and even bilberries, depending on the species. Nearly all are native except *V. macrocarpon*, the common cranberry.

**Use:** The fruits are edible.

**Range:** Vacciniums are forest inhabitors, found mostly in the western part of the state and farther into the Northwest. They are found in woodland clearings and in the woods themselves, mostly coniferous woods. They like moist and shaded areas and north-facing hills.

**Similarity to toxic species:** None

**Best time:** Early spring for flowers; early summer for fruit

**Status:** Common

**Tools needed:** Collecting basket

## PROPERTIES

These are shrubs with alternate evergreen to deciduous leaves, which are broadly lance shaped. The stems are trailing to erect. The flower's petals generally number four to five, with a corolla that is cup or urn shaped. The fruit could be red or blue, larger or smaller, and have flattened ends. Generally, the plants with the most desirable fruits are the smaller shrubs, about 3 feet tall, with the larger sweet, juicy blueberries measuring about ¼ to ½ inch in diameter.

The fruits of all *Vaccinium* species can be eaten, and some are better than others. The best way to make sure you have identified the plant is to observe it when the plant is fruiting, and then take note of the leaf and stem characteristics.

Many species grow in the Northwest, and they are loosely categorized into three groups: those that are found in the bogs and swamps; those that produce the tiny (usually) red berries, which are very sweet but require a lot of time to collect in any appreciable amount (for example, *V. scoparium*, or whortleberry); and those that grow in the higher elevations where there is well-drained soil, with dark blue berries, such as *V. globulare*.

Fruit and leaf of *Vaccinium ovatum* LILY JANE TSONG

## HUCKLEBERRY, EVERGREEN
*Vaccinium ovatum*

This is an evergreen shrub with hairy leaves, 2–5 centimeters long, elliptical to lanceolate, and leathery. The five sepals are fused at the base. The fruit is black, about 6–9 millimeters long. The shrubs grow in the clearings of conifer forests, mostly in the western Cascades. According to some early historians, the Karok waited until fall, preferably after a frost, to eat these purple to black fruits, because they were sweeter then.

On January 27, 1806, Meriwether Lewis wrote: "The natives either eat these berrys when ripe immediately from the bushes or dried in the sun or by means of their sweating kilns; very frequently they pound them and bake them in large loaves of 10 or fifteen pounds; this bread keeps very well during one season and retains the moist jeucies of the fruit much better than by any other method of preservation. This bread is broken and stirred in cold water until it be sufficiently thick and then eaten; in this way the natives most generally use it."

Red huckleberry, *V. parvifolium* KYLE CHAMBERLAIN

## HUCKLEBERRY, RED
### *Vaccinium parvifolium*

This one is deciduous, rarely evergreen, with leaves 10–25 millimeters long, elliptic to ovate, and thin. They are most likely to be found in moist and shaded woodlands of the western Cascades.

These bright red fruits were eaten fresh by the Karok, Pomo, and Bear River Band tribes in midsummer when they ripened.

A handful of red huckleberries KYLE CHAMBERLAIN

The fruit of blueberry, *V. uliginosum* JEAN PAWEK

## BOG BLUEBERRY
*Vaccinium uliginosum*

The fruits of all species can be eaten either raw or cooked. The flavor of the ripe fruit can vary from tart to very sweet. They can be used to makes pies and jellies, cobblers, and preserves. The fruits can also be dried for later use and can be used to make a fruit pemmican.

The dried leaves can be infused to make a tasty and nutritious tea.

# OAK FAMILY (Fagaceae)

The Oak family includes 7 genera and about 900 species worldwide. There are three genera in Washington.

An Oregon oak with acorn JULIE KIERSTEAD NELSON

## OREGON OAK
*Quercus garryana*

There are about 600 species of *Quercus* worldwide, with only the Oregon oak (*Quercus garryana*) found in the wild in Washington. There are also a few nonnative species used for landscaping.

**Use:** Acorns used for food once leached; miscellaneous craft and dye uses

**Range:** Oregon oak is found mostly in the western Cascades.

**Similarity to toxic species:** The tannic acid in acorns is considered "toxic," but it's so bitter that you'd never eat enough to get sick or cause a problem.

**Best time:** Acorns mature from mid-September to as late as early February.

**Status:** Common

**Tools needed:** Collecting bag

## PROPERTIES

Some oak trees are deciduous and some are evergreen; the leaf shapes vary from simple to pinnately lobed.

The fruit of all oak trees is the acorn, which every child can recognize. Some acorns are fat, some long and thin, and the caps can vary significantly. Still, the nut set in a scaly cap is universally recognized as the acorn. You should have no trouble recognizing acorns wherever you live.

## USES

The acorn is a wonderful source of starchy food. Though I have three separate cookbooks devoted

Billy Nickel grinds acorns on a metate. The next step is to leach the ground flour with water and then make pancakes when all the tannic acid is removed.

entirely to using acorns in the modern kitchen, I generally use acorns only for cookies, pancakes, and bread.

In the old days, acorns were typically collected, dried, and then stored until needed. The acorns were then shelled, as they are much easier to shell when dried. They would first be ground up, then placed on a sloping rock with a lip at the lower end, or some other variation of a colander. Cold or hot water poured over the acorn meal would wash out the tannic acid. You'd know it was done by tasting. Then the meal was mostly used as a thickener in soups and stews, making a type of gravy.

Today, on the trail or in the kitchen, the neatest and quickest way to process acorns is to boil them, changing the water repeatedly until they are no longer bitter. Then, after drying, I prefer to process them through a hand-crank meat grinder to produce a coarse meal. For a finer grind, you can use a coffee grinder. Once the meal is dry, it is perfect for any product calling for flour. I typically mix the acorn flour 50/50 with wheat or other flour. This is partly for flavor, and partly because acorn flour doesn't hold together as well as, for example, wheat flour.

The more traditional method of processing involves first shelling the acorns and then grinding them while still raw. I typically do this on a large flat-rock metate. Then the meal is put into some sort of primitive colander, and water (hot or cold) is poured through it. There were many possible ways to create a colander in the old days; today I just put a cotton cloth inside a large colander and pour cold water over it. The water takes a while to trickle out, and it may require several pourings of water before the acorn meal is no longer bitter and can be eaten.

I have had modern acorn products of chips, pound cake, and pasta, and they are delicious. If I have to describe the acorn flavor, I would say that products made with acorn have a subtle graham cracker flavor.

How good are acorns for you? Here are some details from a chart published in *Temalpakh: Cahuilla Indian Knowledge and Usage of Plants* by Lowell John Bean and Katherine S. Saubel. Their source was Martin A. Baumhoff, *Ecological Determinants of Aboriginal California Populations* (Berkeley: University of California Press, 1936, p. 162), as modified by Carl Brandt Wolf, *California Wild Tree Crops* (Claremont, CA: Rancho Santa Ana Botanic Garden, 1945, table 1), and W. S. Spector, *Handbook of Biological Data* (Philadelphia and London: W. B. Saunders Co., 1956, table 156).

## CHEMICAL COMPOSITION OF HULLED ACORNS (IN PERCENT)

| Species | Water | Protein | Fats | Fiber | Carbohydrates | Ash | Total Proteins, Fats, Carbohydrates |
|---|---|---|---|---|---|---|---|
| *Q. lobata* | 9.0 | 4.9 | 5.5 | 9.5 | 69.0 | 2.1 | 79 |
| *Q. garryana* | 9.0 | 3.9 | 4.5 | 12.0 | 68.9 | 1.8 | 77 |
| *Q. kelloggii* | 9.0 | 4.6 | 18.0 | 11.4 | 55.5 | 1.6 | 78 |
| Barley | 10.1 | 8.7 | 1.9 | 5.7 | 71.0 | 2.6 | 82 |
| Wheat | 12.5 | 12.3 | 1.8 | 2.3 | 69.4 | 1.7 | 84 |

### RECIPE

**Northwest Memories**

Use processed acorn flour (with tannic acid removed), mixed half-and-half with wheat flour and an appropriate amount of water. Add a handful of fresh or dried wild berries for flavor.

The dough is then formed into small loaves and cooked on a soapstone slab.

# GOOSEBERRY FAMILY (Grossulariaceae)

This family includes only the *Ribes* genus. There are 120 species worldwide, with at least 21 in Washington, not including varieties. These are found in all environments. Forest species are generally not terribly palatable, and some are without significant pulp. These include *R. acerifolium, R. bracteosum, R. divaricatum, R. hudsonianum, R. inerme, R. lacustre, R. laxiflorum, R. lobbii, R. montigenum, R. niveum, R. oxyacanthoides, R. rubrum, R. sanguineum, R. triste, R. velutinum, R. viscosissimum, R. watsonianum,* and *R. wolfii.*

Ripe currants. Note the dried-up old flower still adhering to the end of the fruit.

## CURRANTS AND GOOSEBERRIES
*Ribes* spp.

**Use:** The fruits are eaten raw, dried, or cooked/processed into juice, jam, and jelly.

**Range:** Found in the mountains, in flat plains, along rivers, etc.

**Similarity to toxic species:** When seeing currants for the first time, some folks think they're looking at poison oak—they've heard the saying "Leaflets three, let it be." But the currant has three lobes per leaf, not three distinct leaflets, as does poison oak.

**Best time:** The fruits are available in mid-spring.

**Status:** Common locally

**Tools needed:** None

Ripe currants

## PROPERTIES

Currants and gooseberries are both the same genus, so we'll treat them together. Both are low shrubs, mostly long vining shoots that arise from the base. Gooseberries have thorns on the stalks and fruits, but currants do not.

The leaves look like little three- to five-fingered mittens. The fruits of both currants and gooseberries hang from the stalks, with the withered flower usually still adhering to the end of the fruit.

You will find currants and gooseberries throughout the diverse ecosystems of Washington.

## USES

Though the straight shoots of currants make excellent arrow shafts, currants and gooseberries are mostly regarded as a great fruit, either eaten raw as a snack, dried, or cooked into various recipes.

Gooseberries are a bit more work to eat since they're covered with tiny spines. I have mashed them and then strained the pulp through a sieve or fine colander. Then I used the pulp as a topping for pancakes.

Currants require no preparation, so they can be picked off the stalks and eaten fresh. But make sure they are ripe—they'll be a bit tart otherwise.

The semi-erect vines of the currant, and the three-lobed leaves

In the old days, the currant was a valuable fruit, dried and powdered and added to dried meats as a sugar preservative. Today you can just dry the fruits into simple trail snacks. Or you can collect a lot and make jams or jellies, even delicious drinks. And though the currant leaf is not usually regarded as an important food source, some can be eaten in salads or in cooked dishes for a bit of vitamin C. They are a bit tough as they get older.

Rule of thumb on the *Ribes* fruits: If it tastes good, it's good to eat. None are poisonous, but not all are palatable.

Currant in the field RICK ADAMS

## CAUTIONS
Be sure you've identified currant or gooseberry, and that you can tell the difference between these and poison oak.

## LEWIS AND CLARK
On April 16, 1805, Meriwether Lewis wrote: "Among others there is a currant which is now in blume and has yellow blossom something like the yellow currant of the Missouri but it is a different species." Botanists believe that Lewis was describing *R. aureum*. Lewis also wrote: "I find these fruits very pleasant particularly the yellow currant which I think vastly preferable to those of our gardens. . . . The fruit is a berry. . . . It is quite as transparent as the red current [*sic*] of our gardens, not so ascid, & more agreeably flavored."

# MINT FAMILY (Lamiaceae)

The Mint family has about 230 genera and about 7,200 species worldwide. In Washington, we have examples from twenty-eight genera, many of which are food and medicine.

Close-up of a wild mint

## MINT
*Mentha* spp.

There are eighteen species of *Mentha* worldwide, with seven found in Washington.

**Use:** As a beverage

**Range:** Along rivers and wet areas; often cultivated and escaping cultivation

**Similarity to toxic species:** None

**Best time:** Mint can be collected at any time.

**Status:** Not common

**Tools needed:** None

Cluster of wild mint growing along a stream JEFF MARTIN

## PROPERTIES
Our wild mints in Washington include spearmint (*M. spicata*), peppermint (*M. piperita*), and field mint (*M. arvensis*). Of our state's seven wild mints, four are natives. In the wild, mints are typically found along streams. They are sprawling, vining plants with squarish stems and finely wrinkled opposite leaves. Crush the

leaf for the unmistakable clue to identification. If you have a good sense of smell, you'll detect the obvious minty aroma.

Peppermint and spearmint are usually cultivated in gardens. They sometimes escape cultivation and are found in marshes, ditches, meadows, around lakes, and in other moist areas.

The white, pink, or violet flowers of *Mentha* are clustered in tight groups along the stalk, often appearing like balls on the stems. The flowers, though five-petaled, consist of an upper two-lobed section and a lower three-lobed section.

## USES

The wild mints are not primarily a food, but are excellent sources for an infused tea. Put the fresh leaves into a cup or pot, boil some water, and then pour the water over the leaves. Cover the cup and let it sit a while. I enjoy the infusion plain, but you might prefer to add honey or lemon or some other flavor.

We've had some campouts where we had very little food and were relying on fishing and foraged food. Even in off-seasons in the mountains, we were able to find wild mint and make a refreshing tea. The aroma is invigorating, and helps to open the sinuses. The flavor and taste of mint tea seems even more enjoyable when camping. Also, you can just crush some fresh leaves and add them to your canteen while hiking. It makes a great cold trail beverage and requires no sweeteners.

Sometimes we add the fresh leaves to trout while it is cooking. They add a great flavor. If used sparingly, you can dice up the fresh leaves and add them to salads for a refreshing minty flavor. Of course they can be diced and added to various dessert dishes, such as ice cream, sherbet, etc. Or you can try adding a few sprigs of mint to your soups and stews to liven up the flavor. And if you really want to try something special for your doomsday parties, add a little fresh mint to your favorite pouch of MRE.

If you have a mildly upset stomach, try some mint tea before reaching for that fizzy pill. Mint tea has a well-deserved reputation for calming an upset stomach. The Ojibwa people used the tea to help reduce fevers.

# MALLOW FAMILY (Malvaceae)

The Mallow family includes 266 genera and about 4,025 species worldwide. There are ten genera represented in Washington, including hibiscus.

According to Dr. Leonid Enari, the Mallow family is a safe family for wild-food experimentation. He cautions, however, that some species may be too fibrous to eat.

The fruits of mallow, also called "cheeses"

## MALLOW
*Malva neglecta*

There are thirty to forty species of *Malva* worldwide, with four found in Washington.

**Use:** Leaves raw, cooked, or dried (for tea); "cheeses" eaten raw or cooked; seeds cooked and eaten like rice

**Range:** Urban areas such as fields, disturbed soils, and gardens

**Similarity to toxic species:** None

**Best time:** Spring

**Status:** Common and widespread

**Tools needed:** None

## PROPERTIES

With their rounded leaves, the plants resemble geraniums. Each leaf's margin is finely toothed, and there is a cleft in the middle of the leaf to which the long stem is attached. If you look closely, you'll see a red spot where the stem meets the leaf.

The flowers are small but attractive, composed of five petals, generally colored white to blue, though some could be lilac or pink. The flowers are followed by the round flat fruits, which gave rise to the plant's other name, "cheeseweed."

These plants are indeed widespread, mostly in urban terrain and on the fringes.

Mallow plant in the field

## USES

When you take a raw leaf and chew on it, you will find it becomes a bit mucilaginous. For this reason, it is used to soothe a sore throat. In Mexico you can find the dried leaf under the Spanish name *malva* at herb stores, sold as a medicine for coughs and sore throats.

Though the entire plant is edible, the stalks and leaf stems tend to be a bit fibrous, so I just use the leaf and discard the stem. These are good added to salads, though most people find them a bit tough as the only salad ingredient.

The mallow leaf is also good in cooked dishes—soups, stews, or finely chopped for omelets and stir-fries. I have even seen some attempts to use larger mallow leaves

Urban farmer Julie Balaa next to a tall mallow that "volunteered" in her orchard

as a substitute for grape leaves in dolmas, which is cooked rice wrapped in a grape leaf. I thought it worked out pretty well.

Another innovative way to prepare these leaves is to sauté them in oil and eat them like "chips."

As this plant flowers and matures, the flat, round seed clusters appear. When still green, these make a good nibble. The green "cheeses" (as they are commonly called) can be added raw to salads, cooked in soups, or even pickled into capers. Once the plant is fully mature and the leaves are drying up, you can collect the now-mature cheeses. The round clusters will break up into individual seeds, which you can winnow and then cook like rice. Though the cooked seeds are a bit bland, they are reminiscent of rice. Because mallow is so very common, it would not be hard to prepare a dish of the mallow seed. To really improve the flavor, try mixing the mallow seeds with quinoa, buckwheat groats, or couscous.

The root of the related marsh mallow (*Althaea officinalis*) was once the source for making marshmallows, which are now just another junk food. Originally the roots were boiled until the water was gelatinous. The water would be whipped to thicken it and then sweetened. You'd then have a spoonful to treat a cough or sore throat. Yes, you can use the common mallow's roots to try this, though it doesn't get quite as thick as the original.

The mallow flower

Explorer Ben Hererra examining the mallow leaf

## MINER'S LETTUCE FAMILY (Montiaceae)

The Miner's Lettuce family includes 22 genera with about 230 species world-wide. There are at least six genera represented in Washington.

Dr. Leonid Enari regarded this as a completely safe family for wild-food experimentation. He taught that all members could be eaten, usually raw, but sometimes needing to be steamed or cooked for improved palatability. Dr. Enari also taught that the seeds of most could be harvested and eaten.

Spring beauty in flower. PHOTO BY KEIR MORSE

## SPRING BEAUTY
### *Claytonia lanceolata*

There are twenty-seven species of *Claytonia* worldwide, with twelve found in Washington (not including subspecies). Many species are found throughout forest habitats: *C. arenicola*, *C. cordifolia*, *C. exigua*, *C. lanceolata*, *C. megarhiza*, *C. parviflora*, *C. perfoliata*, *C. rubra*, *C. sibirica*, *C. washingtoniana*. This genus was formerly referred to as *Montia*.

Spring beauty. PHOTO BY BOB SWEATT

**Use:** Entire plant, including the bulbs, can be eaten.

**Range:** Widespread from Canada, east to the Rockies, south to central California. In Washington, expect to find it mostly in open fields and subalpine meadows, mainly in the Cascades.

**Similarity to toxic species:** None

**Best time:** Spring. It's one of the first spring plants that can be eaten.

**Status:** Relatively common locally

**Tools needed:** Bag for leaves, trowel for tubers

## PROPERTIES

Spring beauty is a perennial herb that grows no more than about 6 inches tall. There is a little root—like a small radish up to 1 inch in diameter. One or more stalks will grow from each little bulb.

The leaves are all more or less basal, appearing in the spring and summer. The linear to lance-shaped leaves are 2½–4 inches long, and are arranged opposite each other. Remember, this is related to miner's lettuce, and the color, texture, and feel of the spring beauty leaves are very much like its relative. The small white flowers often have pink veins and are 5–12 millimeters wide.

Spring beauty is found mostly in subalpine areas, even at the edges of snowmelt. This is a wilderness plant, not one you'll find in urban fields or in your backyard. Once, however, when pulled over to the side of the road at a high-elevation location, I found spring beauty growing in a little patch of moist soil between the road and the abutting mountain.

## USES

Spring beauty leaves are pleasant to all palates and can be used as a main salad ingredient or mixed with other greens. They are also great just cooked like spinach. You can try them in egg dishes and soups. The flavor is mild and the texture is spinach-like, so these greens will go well with most dishes.

The little starchy bulbs can be dug, but I generally just leave them alone. In heavily traveled areas, I have seen certain wild foods "dry up" until the area has had a chance to recover. Yes, these bulbs are good—mild, tasty, and nutritious. The bulbs are down about 6 inches at least, and you can carefully dig them out with a little trowel.

But be an ecological forager. Don't deplete a patch; do your best to keep the area looking natural, and leave it better than when you found it!

## LEWIS AND CLARK

As most Washingtonians know, the Lewis and Clark Expedition passed along the Columbia River and dipped into Oregon. According to the journal kept by Captain Lewis, in an entry dated June 25, 1806: "I met with a plant the root of which the Shoshones eat. It is a small knob root a good deel in flavor and consistency like the Jerusalem artichoke." He was speaking of the spring beauty tubers.

Very young miner's lettuce plant

## MINER'S LETTUCE and SIBERIAN MINER'S LETTUCE
*Claytonia perfoliata* and *C. sibirica*

There are twenty-seven species of *Claytonia* worldwide, with twelve found in Washington (not including subspecies). This genus was formerly referred to as *Montia*.

**Use:** Entire aboveground plant can be eaten raw, boiled, steamed, sautéed, or added to soup, eggs, etc.

**Range:** Mostly found in moist canyons below 3,000 feet, on both sides of the Cascades, with *C. perfoliata* more common

**Similarity to toxic species:** None

**Best time:** Spring

**Status:** Common seasonally

**Tools needed:** None

## PROPERTIES

Miner's lettuce was one of the very first wild foods that I learned to identify. I'd seen the characteristic leaf—a round cuplike leaf with the flower stalk growing out of the middle—in Bradford Angier's *Free for the Eating*. It was just one

Flowering miner's lettuce appears as a cup-shaped leaf with the flower stalk arising from the middle of the "cup." RICK ADAMS

drawing, but I was certain I'd be able to recognize it. One day I got a phone call from a fellow budding forager, and he told me that he'd spotted the plant in the local mountains. I bicycled to the site that afternoon, climbed up the hillside, and, sure enough, I found it!

That night I tried my first miner's lettuce in salad and some boiled like spinach. It was good, but perhaps the experience was a bit anticlimactic because I was so wrapped up in the lore and history of the plant. I didn't realize there'd be nothing really incredible about the plant—just a tasty though somewhat bland leaf that could be used in many ways.

Miner's lettuce leaves are formed in a rosette, with each leaf arising from the root. The young leaves are linear; the older ones are somewhat triangular to quadrangular in shape, with some appearing water-spotted. The key characteristic

Miner's lettuce plant in the field RICK ADAMS

is the flowering stalk with its pink or white five-petaled flowers, which arise from a cup-shaped leaf. Clusters of these unique cup-shaped leaves, all arising from a common root, like a head of leaf lettuce, make this a very easy plant to recognize.

## USES

It seems that everyone knows miner's lettuce. This is probably because the plant is so distinctive—when it's in flower, you really can't confuse it for something else. Plus, it tastes good, often grows very abundantly, and is easy to work with. Think of the plant as a somewhat succulent lettuce that is also good when cooked, and you'll get some idea how versatile this plant can be.

Flavor- and texture-wise, this is perhaps one of my favorite wild

A student examines the unique miner's lettuce plant.

foods. My brother Richard always regarded it as his favorite. We have used it in many recipes—just think of all the diverse ways in which we use common spinach!

BOTANICAL UPDATE: Botanists now prefer the earlier name, Indian lettuce, rather than miner's lettuce, in recognition of the Native Americans who used this plant and taught the incoming miners about it.

To give some examples of the many ways in which we can eat miner's lettuce, consider a weekend survival trip I once led for a dozen young men. Our only food was what we fished or foraged, and there was very little growing in the area besides miner's lettuce. We had miner's lettuce salad, miner's lettuce soup, fried miner's lettuce, boiled miner's lettuce, miner's lettuce cooked with fish, and miner's lettuce broth! If we were in a kitchen with all sorts of condiments, we'd have had miner's lettuce omelets, and soufflés, and stir-fries, and green drinks.

In other words, in any recipe—raw, cooked, or juiced—that calls for "greens," you can use miner's lettuce.

## RECIPE

**Richard's Salad**

This is my brother Richard's recipe. He lived in Portland for part of the year, working as a welder for the Rose Festival, and made miner's lettuce salads whenever possible in the spring.

Rinse 4 cups of miner's lettuce leaves. Mix with a dressing of equal parts cold-pressed olive oil and raw apple cider vinegar, to which you can add a dash of garlic powder and paprika, to taste. Richard sometimes topped his salad with sliced hard-boiled eggs.

# EVENING PRIMROSE FAMILY (Onagraceae)

The Evening Primrose family has 22 genera and about 657 species worldwide. There are sixteen genera of this family in Washington.

Fireweed flowers RON AND ANTHONY BANIAGA

## FIREWEED
### Chamerion angustifolium

There are two species of *Chamerion* in Washington. This genus was formerly known as *Epilobium*.

**Use:** Leaves and tender portions are edible.

**Range:** Widespread, though more common in western Washington

**Similarity to toxic species:** Could be confused with other plants when not in flower, but when fireweed is in flower, it cannot be confused with anything else.

**Best time:** Spring

**Status:** Common in certain areas, especially in burned or clear-cut areas. A known fire-follower.

**Tools needed:** Clippers to collect tender stems

## PROPERTIES

The flowering fireweed is very conspicuous and somewhat emblematic of the Pacific Northwest.

As the common name implies, fireweed is a fire-follower, often sprouting up in large patches in areas that have recently burned. The species name *angustifolium* ("narrow-leaved") is constructed from the Latin words *angustus* for "narrow" and *folium* for "leaf."

The reddish stems of this herbaceous perennial are usually erect, smooth, and from 2 to nearly 8 feet tall. Alternately arranged leaves are lanceolate and more or less pinnately veined. The flowers have four magenta to pink petals, 2–3 centimeters in diameter. The styles have four stigmas, and there are eight stamens.

Fireweed plant in flower SIMON TONGE

Leaves of the fireweed plant RON AND ANTHONY BANIAGA

A patch of fireweed RON AND ANTHONY BANIAGA

The reddish-brown linear seed capsule splits from its apex. It bears hundreds of minute brown seeds, which blow about and spread the plant. Fireweed also spreads by its underground roots, eventually forming a large patch.

## USES

The very youngest shoots can be snapped off and boiled or steamed like asparagus. The young shoots were collected in the spring by various Native peoples and cooked alone or mixed with other greens, which you can do too.

As the plant matures, the leaves become tough and somewhat bitter, but could still be cooked to make more palatable. However, the stems of the older plant can be peeled and eaten raw. Fireweed is a good source of vitamin C and vitamin A.

A tea made from the mature leaves has been used as a laxative. Blackfoot people crushed the root and made it into a poultice to treat various skin problems like burns, cuts, and abrasions.

Various candies and jellies, and even ice cream, are made today in Alaska from the fireweed plant. Okay, so the jelly is not a "health food," but you might be able to tweak the recipe somehow and use a better sugar.

## RECIPE

### Fireweed Jelly

Gakona Baby of Alaska makes several batches of fireweed jelly each summer when fireweed is in bloom. Gakona says it is important that only the blooms be harvested, and not the stems. Also, she has tried this recipe with Certo, and it does not set, so be sure to use Sure-Jell or a powdered pectin.

2½ cups fireweed juice (see below)
1 teaspoon lemon juice
½ teaspoon butter
1 (1¾-ounce) package dry pectin
3 cups sugar

Begin by making fireweed juice. Harvest about 8 packed cups of fireweed flowers; rinse thoroughly and put in a 2-quart pot. Add just enough water so the water level is just below the top of the flowers. When finished, the juice should be a deep purple color—if it is brownish, too much water was used in the boiling process. Boil the flowers in water until the color is boiled out and the petals are a grayish color. Ladle the juice into a jar through a cheesecloth to strain.

Warm the fireweed juice, lemon juice, and butter on the stovetop. Add the pectin, bring to a boil, and boil hard for 1 minute.

Add the sugar and bring to a full boil for 1 minute. Skim the top of the jelly. Pour into a pitcher (making it easier to fill the jars) and skim again. Fill sterilized jars, leaving ⅛ inch of space at the top. Process in a hot water bath for 10 minutes.

Yields four 8-ounce jars.

—Recipe from Gakona Baby

# OXALIS FAMILY (Oxalidaceae)

Though the Oxalis family contains 5 genera and 880 species worldwide, in Washington it is represented only by the *Oxalis* genus.

The yellow flowers and leaves of the native *Oxalis suksdorfii* JEFFEREY BARRETT

## SOUR GRASS, aka WOOD SORREL
*Oxalis* spp.

There are up to 950 species of *Oxalis* worldwide. At least six are found in Washington.

**Use:** Everything can be used. Aboveground leaves and stems can be eaten raw, cooked, or pickled. The tiny tubers can also be eaten cooked.

**Range:** Some are very common in urban settings; others are found in mountains, meadows, and fields.

**Similarity to toxic species:** None

**Best time:** Generally, spring

**Status:** Common in urban areas

**Tools needed:** None

Oxalis leaves emerging from the forest floor in Washington JULIA HAN

## PROPERTIES

Sour grass is widespread, and most gardeners dislike it because it is such a successful plant. It spreads and spreads; if it grows in your yard, there's probably much more than you're likely to use for food.

The leaves arise from thin stems, and each leaf appears to be three hearts connected at the apex of the hearts. Many leaves appear to be water-spotted. The flower stalks are typically taller than the leaves. Flower colors vary from white to pink to yellow. If you dig around under the plant, you'll see some of the tiny tubers of the plant, typically no bigger than a pea.

This is one of the plants commonly referred to as a shamrock, or "four-leaf clover." However, oxalis is not a clover and is not related to clover. Typically, each leaf of oxalis is divided into the three heart-shaped leaflets, though you will occasionally find four leaflets.

## USES

Yes, this makes a good trail nibble, but you really can't eat a lot—it's just too sour because of the plant's oxalic acid. But everyone likes this plant. Children rarely refuse sour grass. It's a great snack, and livens up other foods.

Use the leaves sparingly in salads for a vinegar flavor. I prefer the flower stalks, but everything aboveground

One of the small oxalis tubers

Oxalis leaves have the appearance of three hearts joined at the apex.

*Oxalis oregana* JEAN PAWEK

can be used. Everything aboveground can also be cooked into soups or stews, but again, add it sparingly. If it's a bit too strong, boil the plant, rinse the water, and then use.

I've had some fermented sour grass that was made just as you'd make sauerkraut with cabbage. Though it was very stringy, it was still tasty.

FORAGER NOTE: A variety of Oxalis called oca (O. tuberosa) has long been cultivated in its native Peru, Bolivia, and Ecuador. These tubers measure just a few inches and are very acidic when fresh. They are dried in the sun for a few days to improve the flavor. When they are dried for a few weeks, the flavor is said to resemble figs. At the very least, when you see the little tubers under the Washington species, you can try them as a nibble, or experiment with cooking or drying them.

# LOPSEED FAMILY (Phrymaceae)

The Lopseed family contains 15 genera worldwide, with 230 species. In Washington, there are five genera of this family.

Monkey flower plant growing in the slow-moving water of a stream

## YELLOW MONKEY FLOWER
*Erythranthe guttata* (formerly *Mimulus guttatus*

(The genus *Mimulus* had formerly been classified within the Figwort family.)

This group is currently undergoing revision as botanists are carefully examining it. Formerly *Mimulus*, there are twenty-two identified species of *Erythranthe* in Washington.

**Use:** Everything tender above the water line

**Range:** Found in slow-moving waters or ponds, up to timberline

**Similarity to toxic species:** None

**Best time:** Spring

**Status:** Common in some areas; not particularly widespread

**Tools needed:** None

## PROPERTIES

This common yellow wildflower grows along the shallow banks of streams, in much the same environment as watercress. It's usually very conspicuous when in flower and fairly easy to recognize.

The bright yellow flowers are typically on a raceme, with five or so flowers per stalk. The flower is composed of an upper lip with two lobes and a lower lip with three lobes, which also may have many red to brown spots or just one large spot. The opening to the tubular flower is hairy. The leaves are opposite, round to oval in shape, usually with irregular teeth.

Yellow monkey flower blossom LILY JANE TSONG

The plant may be an annual or perennial, with the stems either erect or sprawling in the water. It's a highly variable plant.

## USES

Since the yellow monkey flower grows in slow-moving waters, make sure the water is clean if you plan to use it in salads.

I've used the leaves and tender stems in salads many times, and I just pinch off the tender above-water sections. The texture is good and the flavor is mild to

Close-up of a yellow monkey flower blossom
LILY JANE TSONG

Monkey flower plant

bland, so it makes a good addition to salads, either alone or mixed with a variety of other wild greens for a balanced flavor. Add some tomatoes and avocado too. Of course, I nearly always add salad dressing to make it tasty, and the salad will have the flavor of whatever salad dressing you use.

The greens also lend themselves well to various cooked dishes. You can simply boil them like spinach, or you can try stir-frying with other greens and vegetables. Yellow monkey flower is mild and can always go into any soup- or stewpot.

# PLANTAIN FAMILY (Plantaginaceae)

The Plantain family has 110 genera and approximately 2,000 species worldwide. There are eighteen genera found in Washington.

Note the seed spikes in this broadleaf plantain.

## PLANTAIN
*Plantago major* and *P. lanceolata*

There are about 250 species of *Plantago* worldwide, with about 11 found in Washington.

**Use:** Young leaves used for food; seeds used for food and medicine
**Range:** Prefers lawns, fields, and wet areas
**Similarity to toxic species:** None
**Best time:** Spring for the leaves; late summer for the seeds
**Status:** Fairly common
**Tools needed:** None

## PROPERTIES

Plantain is as common an urban weed as dandelion, though not as widely known. It's usually found in lawns and fields, but also in wet areas.

All the leaves radiate from the base in a rosette fashion, with the basal leaves typically from about 2 to 6 inches in length. *P. lanceolata*'s leaves are narrow, prominently ribbed with parallel veins. *P. major* has broad glabrous leaves, up to 6 inches long, roundish or ovate in shape. Both have leaves that are covered with short soft hairs.

The flowers are formed in spikes (somewhat resembling a miniature cattail flower spike), usually just a few inches long, and on stems that are typically no more than 1 foot tall. Each greenish flower is composed of four sepals, a small corolla, and four

A larger-than-usual broadleaf plantain leaf

stamens (sometimes two). The flowers are covered by dry, scarious bracts. When the spikes are dry, you can strip off the seeds and winnow them.

## USES

The young tender leaves of spring are the best to eat; use in salads or as you would spinach. Leaves that have become more fibrous with age need longer cooking, and they are best finely chopped or pureed and cooked in a cream sauce. The leaves have a mild laxative effect.

The seeds can be eaten once cleaned by winnowing. They can be ground into flour and used as you would regular flour, or soaked in water (to soften) and then cooked like rice. Once cooked, the seeds are slightly mucilaginous and bland. They can be eaten

Broadleaf plantain

Narrowleaf plantain

Narrowleaf plantain with its seed spikes

plain or flavored with honey, butter, or other seasoning.

Cooked plantain leaves have been used as a direct poultice on boils. Plantain is a vulnerary (promotes healing) and is noted for its styptic, antiseptic, and astringent qualities. Native peoples used the cooked leaves as a poultice for wounds.

Plantain leaf, crushed or chopped and used as a poultice, is perhaps the best herb to use for puncture wounds to the body (knife wound, stepping on a nail, etc.). Early American colonists used plantain on insect and venomous reptile bites, and used the seeds for expelling worms.

Narrowleaf plantain by the side of the road

The asymmetrical veronica flower

## VERONICA, aka SPEEDWELL
*Veronica americana*
The *Veronica* genus has about 250 species worldwide, 18 of which are found in Washington.

**Use:** The entire plant (tender stems and leaves) above the root can be eaten.
**Range:** Grows in slow-moving waters, in the same environment as watercress
**Similarity to toxic species:** None
**Best time:** Spring and summer
**Status:** Somewhat common
**Tools needed:** None

### PROPERTIES
*Veronica americana* is a native and is frequently confused with watercress because they both grow in water. I admit to the superficial resemblance, but there really are some obvious differences. Veronica has a simple leaf about 1–2 inches long, whereas watercress has pinnately divided leaves very much like many of the members of the Mustard family. Watercress has a typical mustard flower formula with the four petals arranged like a cross, and its color is white. But the veronica flower is lavender and asymmetrical with four petals, the upper one being wider than the others.

A veronica arising from a bed of watercress

Several veronica plants in this stream's slowly moving waters

## USES

If I have no concerns about the water's safety from which I've picked the veronica, I add it to salads. It is not strongly flavored, and you can use the entire plant. Just pinch it off at water level (no need to uproot the plant), rinse it, and then dice it into your salad. No need to pick off just the leaves—eat the entire above-water plant. Since it's so bland, you can mix it with stronger-flavored greens in your salad. It goes well with watercress, as well as any of the mustards.

Veronica also goes well with soup dishes and stir-fries. It never gets strongly bitter, like watercress, and it never really gets fibrous. It's a mild plant that's fairly widespread in waterways.

If you live near a waterway where veronica grows, you'll find that it's a good plant to use in a variety of dishes where you might otherwise include spinach. Try some gently sautéed with green onions, and add some eggs to make an omelet. Try a cream soup in which you've gently cooked some veronica greens.

# BUCKWHEAT FAMILY (Polygonaceae)

The Buckwheat family has 48 genera and about 1,200 species worldwide. Eleven of these genera are found in Washington.

Flower of the American bistort DEBRA COOK

## AMERICAN BISTORT
### Bistorta bistortoides

The genus *Bistorta* includes two species in Washington. This plant was formerly referred to as *Polygonum bistortoides*.

**Use:** Edible leaf, root, and seed

**Range:** Moist meadows and forest clearings, from the foothills to above timberline

**Similarity to toxic species:** When not in flower, could easily be confused with another, possibly toxic plant

**Best time:** Leaves and roots in spring; seeds in late summer

**Status:** Common

**Tools needed:** Trowel

American bistort plant showing leaves, stems, and flowers DEBRA COOK

American bistort in the field BOB SWEATT

## PROPERTIES

These are perennial herbs with stems rising from 2 to 8 feet tall. Leaves have long stalks, with the blade up to 6 inches long. Most of the leaves are basal, and the leaves that appear on the flower stalks are shorter and thinner. The leaves are elliptic to lanceolate-oblong. The rhizomes are contorted.

## USES

All members of *Bistorta* are edible, though palatability varies. The root of *B. bistortoides* can be eaten raw or cooked (boiled, baked, and roasted). The flavor is somewhat like a chestnut.

The seeds—as with all the members of this genus and family—can be used for food. They are generally best winnowed and ground, and then cooked into a hot mush or some sort of bread or biscuit.

The leaves are also okay to eat, though you should use only the very young leaves for salads. The leaves can also be steamed or boiled and served like spinach, or added to soups, stews, egg and rice dishes, etc.

## LEWIS AND CLARK

In the journals of their expeditions, Lewis and Clark described where they found American bistort: "in moist grounds on the quamash flats." They did not say whether they ate any.

Mountain sorrel plant with seed spike HAGAN

# MOUNTAIN SORREL
*Oxyria digyna*
There are four species of *Oxyria*; apparently, only this species is found in Washington.

**Use:** Edible leaves and seeds
**Range:** Found throughout the Cascades and Olympic Mountains in the subalpine and alpine areas
**Similarity to toxic species:** None
**Best time:** Spring and summer
**Status:** Sporadic
**Tools needed:** Collecting bag

## PROPERTIES

This plant seems to prefer the harsher environment of higher elevations, never growing in massive stands, but a little here, a little there. It's relatively easy to recognize and collect a few leaves for your meal.

This is a perennial herb with mostly basal leaves. The leaves are heart shaped to kidney shaped, about 2 inches across and on a stem that's 3–4 inches long. The erect stem rises no more than 8–10 inches tall.

If you're familiar with the other members of this family, like dock or sheep sorrel, you'll probably notice the family resemblance. The flowers are also typical of this family, with many green to reddish flowers clustered on the stalk, which rises about 1 foot tall. There are four perianth segments, with the outer two spreading. There are six stamens and two red stigmas. When the seeds mature in the fall, they will be more conspicuously red, flat, and winged like the dock seeds.

Mountain sorrel plant STEVE MATSON

## USES

Mostly found in the higher elevations, this isn't a backyard plant. You might add some to a meal when out hiking or backpacking.

The leaves are tart, like sheep sorrel, and are great added to salads. Try them with an avocado salad. They're also good in a mixed salad. The leaves are a great addition to stews, soups, freeze-dried meals, MREs, etc.

The flavor is very much like oxalis or sour grass, so you'll be adding this to other recipes, not making dishes from it alone. A handful of the leaves makes a tart addition to soups cooked up on the trail.

Close-up of the mountain sorrel seeds
STEVE MATSON

Patch of sheep sorrel

## SHEEP SORREL
*Rumex acetosella*

There are 190–200 species of *Rumex* worldwide, with at least 17 in Washington, not counting varieties or subvarieties.

**Use:** The leaves are good raw in salads and can also be added to various cooked dishes.
**Range:** Found in the higher elevations, often around water, and often near disturbed soils and in urban areas
**Similarity to toxic species:** None
**Best time:** Spring to early summer
**Status:** Can be abundant locally
**Tools needed:** None

## PROPERTIES
Sheep sorrel is native to Europe and Asia. It is common and widespread, and is recognized by its characteristic leaves, which are generally basal, lance to oblong shaped, with the base tapered to hastate or sagittate. In other words, it looks like an elongated arrowhead. When the seed stalk matures, it is brown, reminiscent of the curly dock seed stalk, but much smaller.

Another patch of sheep sorrel

A student collects sheep sorrel leaves to add to her dinner.

Sheep sorrel leaf LOUIS-M. LANDRY

## USES

Where the plant is common, you can pinch off many of the small leaves to add to salad, or even to use as the main salad ingredient. I've enjoyed sheep sorrel salads with just avocado and dressing added. The leaves are mildly sour, making a very tangy salad.

The flavor is somewhat similar to the leaves of oxalis, though not as strong. They can be effectively added raw to other foods like tostadas (in place of lettuce) or sandwiches. They add a bit of a tang when added to soups and stews, and can be very effective at livening up some MREs.

> RECIPE
>
> **Shiyo's Garden Salad**
>
> Rinse a bowl full of young sheep sorrel leaves. Add at least 1 ripe avocado and 1 ripe tomato, both diced. Toss with some Dr. Bronner's oil-and-vinegar dressing. Eat it outside where the wind can blow your hair.

Curly dock leaves

## CURLY DOCK and BROAD-LEAVED DOCK
*Rumex crispus* and *R. obtusifolius*
There are about 190–200 species of *Rumex* worldwide, with at least 17 in Washington, not counting varieties or subvarieties.

**Use:** Young dock leaves eaten raw or cooked; seeds harvested and added to various flours; stems used like rhubarb
**Range:** Prefers wet areas, but can be found in most environments
**Similarity to toxic species:** None
**Best time:** The leaves are best gathered when young in the spring. Seeds mature in late August, and may be available for months.
**Status:** Common and widespread
**Tools needed:** None

### PROPERTIES
Curly dock is a widespread perennial invasive plant in Washington. It is originally from Europe, and today is found not only in Washington but worldwide. Though it has many good uses, it is often despised and poisoned because it not only survives well but often takes over entire areas.

Young curly dock plant

Rosette of young curly dock leaves. Note the wavy or curly margins of the leaves.

The root looks like a dark orange carrot, and the spring leaves arise directly from the root. The young leaves are long and linear, and curved on their margins. The leaves can be over 1 foot long and pointed.

As the season progresses, the flower stalk arises, and it can reach about 4 feet, even taller in ideal conditions. The seeds are formed with three to each unit, with a papery sheath around the seed. They are green at first and then mature to a beautiful chocolate brown.

## USES

You can make meals from both the leaves and the mature seeds of curly dock. Let's start with the leaves.

Pick only the very youngest leaves for salad, the smaller ones before the plant has begun to send up its seed stalk. These will be not too tough, and the flavor will be sour, somewhat like French sorrel. You can just rinse them, dice them, and add them to salads. I've had *only* these for salad, with dressing and avocado; it was good, but only because the leaves were young.

Older leaves are best boiled like spinach, or—ideally with the midrib removed—sautéed with potatoes and onions. Or you can just add some to soups and stews. The leaves change color and darken a bit with cooking, and the cooking softens the tougher older leaves. But you really want to cook older

William Hartman (of Brier, Washington) in a patch of curly dock

leaves, as they are tougher and bitter and astringent, all of which is reduced somewhat by cooking.

I have seen the brown seed spikes sold in floral supply shops as "fall decoration," and they are very attractive. Those little seeds can be stripped off the stalks with your hands, and then rubbed between the hands to remove the wing from the seed. You don't have to be too picky here, as it can all be used. I blow off the wings and then mix the seed half-and-half with flour for pancakes, and sometimes bread. You could also toss some seed into soup to increase the protein content.

I've seen some folks go to the trouble of winnowing and then further grinding the seeds in a mill to get a fine flour. I never bother, but some folks prefer the finer flour, which is a bit more versatile than the seeds. For example, a fine flour can be mixed half-and-half with wheat, blended, and put through a pasta machine to make a curly dock seed pasta, which tastes really good.

The leaf stems are tart and sour, but often make a good nibble. Young stems can be processed and used like rhubarb for pies.

Each season, dock plants send up seed stalks, which mature to a chocolate color.

## RECIPE

### Curly Dock "Nori" (Vegetable Chips)

Dehydration is a neat way to make some interesting and flavorful ingredients for wild-food dishes. This one is easy to do. You will just need a silicone sheet.

100 grams chopped curly dock
1 garlic clove
½ cup water
2 teaspoons soy sauce
¼ teaspoon salt

Blend all the ingredients and, using a spatula, spread on a silicone sheet. Dehydrate at 160°F until fully dry.

—Recipe from Pascal Baudar

# PURSLANE FAMILY (Portulacaceae)

The Purslane family has recently been redefined by botanists as having only the one genus, with about one hundred species worldwide; only this species is found in Washington. Many of the plants that were formerly in this family are now a part of the Miner's Lettuce family. This family was considered by Dr. Leonid Enari to be entirely safe for consumption.

Purslane, with its round, succulent stem and paddle-shaped leaves

## PURSLANE
*Portulaca oleracea*

**Use:** Entire aboveground plant can be eaten raw, cooked, pickled, etc.

**Range:** Prefers disturbed soils of gardens and rose beds; also found in the sandy areas around rivers

**Similarity to toxic species:** Somewhat resembles prostrate spurge. However, spurge lacks the succulence of purslane. Also, when you break the stem of spurge, a white milky sap appears.

**Best time:** Spring into summer

**Status:** Relatively common

**Tools needed:** None

Purslane in the field

Farmers often collect purslane to sell at farmers' markets, often sold as "verdolaga."

## PROPERTIES

Purslane starts appearing a bit later than most of the spring greens, typically by June or July. It is a very common annual in rose beds and gardens, though I do occasionally see it in the wild, typically in the sandy bottoms around streams.

The stems are succulent, red-colored, and round in the cross section. The stems sprawl outward from the roots, rosette-like, just lying on the ground. The leaves are paddle shaped. The little yellow flower is five-petaled.

## USES

When you chew on a fresh stem or leaf of purslane, you'll find it mildly sour and a bit crunchy. It's really a great snack, though I like it a lot in salads. Just rinse to get all the dirt off, dice, add some dressing, and serve. Add tomatoes and avocado if you have any.

Add it to sandwiches, tostadas, even on the edges of your chiles rellenos and huevos rancheros. I've also eaten it fried, boiled, baked (in egg dishes), and other ways too. It's versatile, tasty, and crisp. It really goes with anything, and it's very nutritious.

If you take the thick stems, clean off the leaves, then cut them into sections of about 4 inches, you can make purslane pickles. There are many ways to make pickles; my way is to simply fill a jar with purslane stems, add raw apple cider vinegar, and let it sit for a few weeks in the refrigerator before eating.

An older purslane plant, largely prostrate, showing round stems and yellow flowers

According to researchers, purslane is one of the richest plant sources of omega-3 fatty acids. That means not only is it good, it's good for you!

## RECIPE

**Purslane Salsa**

2 cups chopped tomatoes
2½ cups chopped foraged purslane
¾ cup chopped onions
3 garlic cloves
1 cup apple cider vinegar
¼ cup sugar
1 large Oregon myrtle leaf
½ cup chopped cilantro and some herbs from the garden (thyme, etc.)
Salt and pepper to taste

Place all the ingredients except the cilantro and herbs in a pot, bring to a boil, and then simmer until the right consistency (light or chunky). Add the cilantro and herbs at the end, and salt and pepper to taste.

Pour into jars, close the lids, and place in the fridge. It should be good for at least a month.

—Recipe from Pascal Baudar

# ROSE FAMILY (Rosaceae)

The Rose family contains 110 genera and 3,000 species worldwide. At least forty-two of these genera are found in Washington.

Serviceberry and fruit JOHN DOYEN

## SERVICEBERRY, aka SASKATOON, JUNEBERRY
*Amelanchier alnifolia*

The *Amelanchier* genus consists of about twenty-five species, only two of which are found in Washington.

**Use:** Edible berries
**Range:** Most common in riparian and moist hillside areas, all the way up to alpine areas
**Similarity to toxic species:** None
**Best time:** Late summer and fall
**Status:** Somewhat common
**Tools needed:** Collecting basket

### PROPERTIES

Serviceberry is a large shrub or small tree with deciduous leaves, often forming dense thickets. There are five varieties of *A. alnifolia*.

The twigs of this native shrub are glabrous, and the leaf is elliptical to round, with obvious serrations, generally serrated above the middle of the leaf. The flowers are five-petaled, white, fragrant, and in clusters of a few to many. The fruit is a pome of two to five papery segments, berrylike, generally spherical, bluish black to purple in color, with a waxy outer skin. Each fruit contains two seeds. The shape somewhat resembles a tiny pomegranate.

## USES

The ripe fruits are good to eat raw, dried, or prepared into jams, etc. Fruits of several species of *Amelanchier* were used for food by various Native American tribes, and all members of this genus are edible. Fruits ripen in late spring into the summer.

Native peoples ate these as fresh fruits, or they dried them for later use. The ripe berries were mashed with water into a paste by the Atsugewi tribe and then eaten fresh. Several of the western tribes were known to dry these fruits and then shape them into loaves for future use.

The berries would remain sweet when dried, and could be reconstituted later when added to water. In some cases, this would be served as a sweet soup. With sugar and flour added, these fruits have been made into a pudding. The fruit can be dried, ground, and used in a pemmican mix.

A closer look at the shape of the fruit and leaf
LOUIS-M. LANDRY

Serviceberry bush in fruit BENNET

Flowering wild strawberries JEAN PAWEK

## STRAWBERRY
*Fragaria* spp.
*Fragaria* contains twenty species worldwide, with five found wild in Washington.

**Use:** Edible berries; leaves used for tea
**Range:** Can be found from beaches up to mountain meadows
**Similarity to toxic species:** None
**Best time:** Spring and summer
**Status:** Widespread
**Tools needed:** Collecting basket

FORAGER NOTE: Strawberry leaf tea (made by infusion), though not strongly flavored, is popular in many circles. It is high in vitamin C and generally used as you'd use blackberry leaf or raspberry leaf tea. It's a mild diuretic and has astringent properties, and is regarded as a tonic for the female reproductive system. When made stronger, the tea is said to be good for hay fever.

Strawberry leaves in the field

## PROPERTIES

If you've grown strawberries in your yard, you will recognize these three wild strawberries:

The beach strawberry (*F. chiloensis*) is found along beaches and coastal grasslands from California north to Alaska. Receptacle is about 10–20 millimeters; leaf petiole is generally 2–20 centimeters.

The wood strawberry (*F. vesca*) is found in partial shade in the forests throughout Washington. Receptacle is about 5–10 millimeters; leaf petiole is generally 3–25 centimeters.

The mountain strawberry (*F. virginiana*) is found in the higher elevations in meadows and forest clearings. Receptacle is about 10 millimeters; leaf petiole is generally 1–25 centimeters.

Their leaves are all basal, generally three-lobed, each leaflet having fine teeth. They look just like the strawberries you grow in your garden, but smaller.

Technically, the strawberry berry is an aggregate accessory fruit, meaning the fleshy part is derived not from the plant's ovaries but from the receptacle that holds the ovaries. In other words, what we call the "fruit" (because, obviously, it looks like a fruit) is the receptacle, and all the little seeds on the outside of the "fruit" are technically achenes—actually one of the ovaries of the flower, with a seed inside it.

Though the wild strawberry prefers higher-elevation forests and clearings, it is found widely throughout the state.

Mature and immature wild strawberry fruit DR. AMADEJ TRNKOCZY

Wild strawberry fruit ZOYA AKULOVA

Wild strawberries are pretty easy to identify. When the average person sees one, especially if it's summer and the plant is in fruit, he or she will typically say, "Hey, look, isn't that a wild strawberry?" Strawberries are so widely known that just about everyone recognizes them when they see them, even though the wild varieties are significantly smaller than the huge ones found in the markets. Cultivated strawberries can get to be about 2—even up to 3—inches long. That's huge! By contrast, a wild strawberry is between ¼ and ½ inch long. A ½-inch wild strawberry is a big one!

Though they may be smaller, wild strawberries are typically sweeter, firmer, and tastier. Yes, it may take longer to collect them, but you'll find that it's worth it.

## USES

You use these in every way that you'd use cultivated strawberries. Eat them as is, dry them, make into jams and jellies, put on top of ice cream and pancakes, etc.

The berries of the beach (or sand) strawberry were eaten by all the coastal Native peoples.

A fruiting branch of *Malus fusca* JEAN PAWEK

## CRABAPPLE
*Malus fusca*

Worldwide, there are about twenty-five species of the *Malus* genus, which includes all of our domestic apples. In Washington, we find at least four species of *Malus*, including *M. pumila* (the domestic apple, and many of its varieties) and the crabapple (*M. fusca*).

**Use:** Edible fruits

**Range:** Occurring chiefly west of the Cascades crest in Washington; Alaska south to California. Found in moist woods, swamps, and open canyons from sea level to moderate elevations in the mountains.

**Similarity to toxic species:** None

**Best time:** Fall through winter

**Status:** Common

**Tools needed:** Collecting basket

## PROPERTIES

If you've ever seen a domestic apple tree in an orchard or backyard, you know what the tree looks like. In the wild, these will be small trees, often in thickets. You'll look at the leaves and the fruit, and you'll say to yourself, "Boy, that sure looks like an apple." Yes, it *is* an apple, a wild apple.

Wild crabapples growing near the Seattle area
WILLIAM J. HARTMAN

A wild crabapple ZOYA AKULOVA

Each leaf is lanceolate to ovate-lanceolate, 4–10 centimeters long, pointed, serrate, occasionally with a lobe on one or both margins, deep green above, paler beneath.

The floral inflorescence typically has five to twelve flowers, and is flat-topped. There are five white petals, twenty stamens (shorter than the petals), and usually three styles.

Do you know what an apple looks like? That's what these look like. They are fleshy, round to obovoid, about 10–16 millimeters long. The color can range from yellow to purplish red.

## USES

If you know what an apple looks like, you'll recognize crabapples, or crabbies. Probably everyone who has seen one for the first time has picked one, chewed on it, and spit it out because it was too sour. These are not great to eat raw like you'd eat a regular domestic apple, but they are still a great find. The first time I saw a crabapple tree was when I was away from home visiting my cousin. We were in an area where the crabapples grew thickly, and I picked one for the first time, recognizing that it was an apple. I bit into it, and thought it was good. "We don't eat those," said my cousin disdainfully. "They give you the runs."

In fact, properly prepared, these can be quite good. I've cooked them, run them through a sieve to get rid of the seeds and skin, and made a great crabapple sauce. You can sweeten with a bit of honey, as you wish.

*Malus fusca* in the field JEAN PAWEK

The fruits can be dried as a snack for later, or mashed and added to other baked goods. The fruits can be cooked, mashed and strained, and used as the basis for an apple drink. Cooking mellows the flavor, but you still might want to add some honey; this goes particularly well with a cinnamon stick.

You can pretty much do anything with crabapples that you'd do with cultivated apples, such as cooking and mashing up a batch, spreading it thin in a pan, and drying it for fruit leather.

If you're good in the kitchen, you can cook up a batch of the small crabapples to make jams or jellies.

The fruits often remain in the trees and will lose a bit of their tartness and even sweeten up a bit if you harvest during wintertime.

Besides the native crabapples, you'd be surprised how many gone-feral apple trees you can find that still produce fruit. Some of the best apples I've ever eaten were picked in orchards that had been abandoned at least a decade earlier, yet they still consistently produced quality fruit.

## CAUTIONS

The seeds of crabapples, and domestic apples, are toxic because of a small amount of a cyanide compound. But you'd have to eat *many* apples to cause sickness, and if you don't chew the seeds, they will just pass through your body. An adult could die if he or she chewed up about ½ cup of pure seed at one sitting. Fortunately, cooking and drying helps break down this chemical, significantly reducing any danger.

Indian plum fruit ZOYA AKULOVA

## INDIAN PLUM
*Oemleria cerasiformis*
There is only one species of *Oemleria*, the Indian plum, which is sometimes also called osoberry.

**Use:** Edible fruits
**Range:** Mostly found west of the Cascades, from Canada down into California. Prefers moist lowlands and stream banks, but can also be found in dry woods.
**Similarity to toxic species:** None
**Best time:** Early summer
**Status:** Widely distributed
**Tools needed:** Collecting bag or basket

### PROPERTIES
The Indian plum is a small tree to large shrub, loosely branched, generally about 5–10 feet tall. Alternately arranged leaves are long and ovate, a bit like an avocado leaf, about 3 inches long, with a unique fruity aroma when crushed. Leaves are deciduous.

A dozen or so white to whitish-green, five-petaled, drooping flowers are found on each stem; there are both male and female plants. The twig is slender, green turning to reddish brown, pith chambered, with conspicuous orange lenticels. The bark is smooth and reddish brown to dark gray in color.

The fruits begin in early spring with an orange color, and mature to blue-black. The fruit is fleshy, and there is a large flattened seed in each one. Of course the fruits form only on the female plants.

## USES

Not everyone likes the flavor of the Indian plum, since it can be bitter and astringent. But the taste varies, and some foragers regard this as one of the better-tasting wild fruits. You can eat these raw, as you'd eat any other fruits, assuming they are palatable. Try them in fruit dishes and salads. When there is a predominant bitterness to the fruits, try them cooked instead.

You can also enjoy these cooked and made into jams, jellies, and pie fillings. Cooking mellows the flavor a bit, and reduces any bitterness that might be present.

Some of the Northwest indigenous peoples ate the fruit and made tea from the bark. Some also chewed on the small twigs, which acted as a mild anesthetic.

Flowers of the Indian plum MATT BELOW

An overview of the Indian plum STEVE MATSON

Immature fruit of the Indian plum STEVE MATSON

Fruit of the wild cherry, *Prunus virginiana*
LOUIS-M. LANDRY

Leaf of the wild cherry, *P. virginiana*
LOUIS-M. LANDRY

## WILD CHERRIES
*Prunus* spp.

There are about 400 species of *Prunus* worldwide, whose common names generally include cherry, almond, apricot, and plum. At least thirteen species of *Prunus* are in Washington. Wild cherries and plums (*Prunus avium, P. cerasifera, P. spinosa,* and *P. domestica*) are widespread in lowlands. *P. armeniaca* can occur in the bunchgrass zone. *P. dulcis* is known to naturalize in the hottest parts of the sagebrush zone. Here, we're primarily concerned with the cherries: chokecherry (*P. virginiana*), bitter cherry (*P. emarginata*), and western chokecherry (*P. virginiana* var. *demissa*).

**Use:** Flesh of the fruit in jams and jellies; meat of the large seed processed into flour

**Range:** Cascades, coastal ranges, riparian, urban fringes

**Similarity to toxic species:** In a sense, this is a toxic plant. The leaves are mildly toxic—see "Cautions," below. And the fruit could get you sick if you eat too much of it raw.

**Best time:** Fruits mature around July into August

**Status:** Common

**Tools needed:** None

Fruit of *Prunus virginiana* MIKE AARON

## PROPERTIES

One way to identify the plant is to crush the leaves, wait a few seconds, and then smell them. They will have a distinct aroma of bitter almond extract, your clue that the leaf contains "cyanide" (hydrocyanic acid).

The fruits are very much like cultivated cherries, except the color is darker red, almost maroon, sometimes even darker. The flesh layer can be very thin in dry years, thicker in the seasons following a good rain. Like domestic cherries, there is a thin shell and the meat inside of the seed.

## USES

The fruit of our wild cherries makes a great trail nibble. I usually see them in August when they ripen, when the trail is hot and dry, and the fruit makes a refreshing treat, if not too sour. But don't eat too much of the raw fruit, or diarrhea might result.

The wild cherry also has a hint of bitterness. The fruit can be cooked off the seeds and the pulp made into jellies, jams, and preserves. You can also make a fruit leather by laying the pulp on a cookie sheet and drying it.

In the old days, Native peoples enjoyed the flesh of the cherry, but they considered the seed to be the most valuable part of the fruit. The seeds were shelled and the inside meat cooked to reduce the cyanide. The cooked seeds, once ground into mush or meal, were then used to make a sweet bread product or added (like acorns) to stews as a gravy or thickening agent.

The bark was boiled by Native peoples and used as a cough and sore throat remedy, as well as for treating diarrhea and headaches.

## CAUTIONS

If you crush the leaf, it will impart a sweet aroma like the bitter almond extract used in cooking. That's the telltale aroma of cyanide, so don't use the leaf for tea.

## LEWIS AND CLARK

On June 11, 1805, Meriwether Lewis became sick and wrote:

> I was taken with such violent pain in the intestens that I was unable to partake of the feast of marrowbones. . . . I directed a parsel of the small twigs [of chokecherry] to be geathered striped of their leaves, cut into pieces of about 2 inches in length and boiled in water until a strong black decoction of an astringent bitter tast was produced; at sunset I took a point [pint] of this decoction and about an hour after repeated the dze. By 10 in the evening I was entirely relieved from pain and in fact every symptom of the disorder forsook me; my fever abated, a gentle perspiration was produced and I had a comfortable and refreshing nights rest.

Wild rose

## WILD ROSE
### *Rosa* spp.

There are about one hundred species of *Rosa* worldwide, which hybridize freely. At least ten species can be found in the wild in Washington, not including varieties, and not including the large array of cultivated roses grown in gardens. The exotics include *R. canina*, *R. eglanteria*, and *R. multiflora*. The natives include *R. pisocarpa*, *R. gymnocarpa*, *R. nutkana*, *R. rugosa*, and *R. woodsii*. All species are widespread at low and middle elevations.

**Use:** Fruits eaten raw or cooked and made into jam or tea; wood useful for arrow shafts

**Range:** Typically riparian, but found in many areas; cultivated roses are common in urban areas.

**Similarity to toxic species:** None (but be wary of eating fruit or flower from roses where commercial fertilizers and insecticides have been used)

**Best time:** Fruits mature in summer.

**Status:** Common

**Tools needed:** Clippers, possibly gloves

Mature wild rose hips

## PROPERTIES

Wild roses are more common than most people think. They are typically found in wet areas, though this is not a fast rule. Wild rose flowers are five-petaled, not the multiple-petaled flowers you find on hybridized roses. After the flowers mature and fade, the fruit develops, often called the "hip," which is usually smaller than a grape. The ripe fruit is bright orange.

The leaves are oddly divided into three, five, or seven petals, and the stalks are covered in thorns. If you've ever had rose bushes in your yard, you have a pretty good idea of what the wild rose looks like.

The wild rose often forms dense thickets. If it gets cut down, or after a burn, there will be many straight shoots in the new growth.

## USES

For food, we have the flower and the fruits. The flowers have long been used to make "rose water" and could also be used to make a mild-flavored infusion. The petals make a flavorful, colorful, and nutritious garnish to soups and salads.

The fruits—commonly called "hips"—are one of the richest sources of vitamin C. The fruits can be eaten fresh, but you should first split them open and scrape out the more fibrous insides. They are typically a bit fibrous, with a hint of bitterness. The fruits are more commonly cooked into a tea or made into jellies.

Some "old-school" archers consider the rose shaft to be one of the finest woods for making arrows, assuming you cut the new straight shoots. You need to then ream the shaft through a rock with a hole in it to remove the thorns.

Close-up of rose hips

## CAUTIONS

Before you eat the petals or fruit, make sure the plants have not been sprayed with any pesticides.

The shoots of wild rose. These were straightened in the past, and were a favorite among Native peoples for arrow shafts.

Flowering blackberry vine LILY JANE TSONG

## BLACKBERRY
*Rubus* spp.
There are about 400–750 species of *Rubus* worldwide, including at least 18 in Washington (not including varieties). These include blackberry, raspberry, and salmonberry, aka thimbleberry (*R. parviflorus*).

**Use:** Berries used for juices, jams, and desserts or dried; leaves used for medicine
**Range:** Riparian and many other areas with sufficient water
**Similarity to toxic species:** Somewhat resembles poison oak, though poison oak lacks the thorns.
**Best time:** Fruits mature in summer.
**Status:** Very common
**Tools needed:** None, but clippers can help.

### PROPERTIES
Even nonbotanists can usually identify the vine and fruit of the very common blackberry. In some parts of Washington, wild blackberries are so common that most go uneaten. Many are regarded nearly as a nuisance. One neighbor encouraged me to pick all I wanted. She described them as "pesky, thorny vines that we can't seem to get rid of." I picked all I could for breakfast and lunch and barely made a dent in the local supply.

The leaves are palmately divided (like a hand) into three, five, or seven segments. The vines are twining on the ground or over low hedges, and are

Note the three-lobed leaves, and the spines on the vine. HELEN WONG

characterized by their thorns, which make it difficult to wade too deep into any of the old hedge-like stands of wild blackberries. The flowers are white, five-petaled, and followed by the fruits, which are aggregate fruits.

Most people instantly recognize the shape of the blackberry because they've seen it in supermarkets or in backyard gardens. The aggregate fruit is a collection of sweet drupelets, with the fruit separating from the flower stalk to form a somewhat hollow, thimble-like shape.

## USES

The blackberry is fairly universally recognized, and everyone who sees the ripe ones ventures out to eat them. I've picked them in the foothills and mountains and along roadsides. The key is to avoid the thorns, and to make sure they are not immature and tart. If the fruit is black, soft, and easily picked—it's ripe! You can eat them right away, or pick a bunch and mash them for a pancake, biscuit, or cake topping. Even better, sprinkle them over a bowl of vanilla ice cream. (Yes, we know that chocolate ice cream is better for you, but the flavor of blackberries clashes a bit with chocolate.)

You could also make a conserve, a jam, a jelly, a pie filling, or a juice. It's

Blackberry fruit

Thimbleberry is a member of the *Rubus* genus. The leaves are much larger than those of blackberries, and the stalks are spineless. The aggregate fruits are similar to a blackberry. JEAN PAWEK

a very versatile berry. And though I rarely have ripe blackberries around long enough to dry them, they can be dried in any food dehydrator and will keep for quite a while. The dried fruits can then be eaten as is or reconstituted for juices or desserts.

An infusion of the leaves has long been used among Native Americans for diarrhea and childbirth pains.

## LEWIS AND CLARK

Lewis and Clark collected a sample of thimbleberry near The Dalles on April 15, 1806. (The site was a major Native American trading center for at least 10,000 years.) Frederick Pursh described the sample as "a shrub of which the natives eat the young Sprout without kooking."

Salmonberry is another member of the *Rubus* genus.
VERNON SMITH

# SAXIFRAGE FAMILY (Saxifragaceae)

There are 38 genera and about 600 species of the Saxifrage family worldwide. These occur mostly in arctic and alpine territories, and some are cultivated. This family is undergoing much study, meaning many of the former classifications are becoming obsolete. According to the latest thinking on this family, at least twenty genera are represented in Washington.

Brook saxifrage plant, with its distinctive kidney-shaped leaves and toothed margins JEAN PAWEK

## BROOK SAXIFRAGE
*Micranthes odontoloma* (formerly *Saxifraga odontoloma, S. arguta*)

There are approximately fifteen species of *Micranthes* found in Washington and nine species of *Saxifraga*, a closely related genus.

**Use:** Leaves are eaten.

**Range:** High mountain areas, typically along streams in alpine areas and wet meadows

**Similarity to toxic species:** None obvious

**Best time:** Best collected in spring into summer

**Status:** Widespread, found from southern Alaska and south into California

**Tools needed:** None

## PROPERTIES

This is a low-growing plant, rising no more than 1 foot or so tall, growing in clusters along streams. It is a herbaceous perennial, with round to kidney-shaped leaves about 3 inches across. Each leaf blade arises from a long stalk and is evenly toothed. The flower stalks rise to about 1½ feet tall, with somewhat inconspicuous white to pink-toned flowers. Each flower consists of five separate, round ephemeral petals, five sepals, ten stamens, and one pistil.

Brook saxifrage plant in flower JEAN PAWEK

In the higher mountain elevations, this is perhaps one of the most common plants you will see. It will be available when there is not much else available at that time or location.

## USES

The flavor is bland, and the texture is ideal for salad. This means it will take on the flavor of whatever you season it with, and you can add it to other greens that are more spicy or bitter in order to mellow them out. They are often available in abundance.

The leaves make an excellent raw salad, especially when collected in the spring. The older leaves become a bit tough and slightly bitter, so should be cooked in soups or stews to tenderize. While these young leaves alone make a good trail salad, it is better blended with other greens and ingredients for a mixed salad.

According to wild-food forager Tom Elpel, "Being nearly tasteless may not seem like a good marketing pitch for an edible wild plant, but in foraging, a lack of flavor is often the most desirable flavor of all. Gather a big bowl of this nearly tasteless salad, then toss in anything else for flavor: a few wild onions, some dandelion leaves, blue violets, aster blossoms, and maybe some clover and strawberry leaves. If you spend much time in the high country, you will quickly become a big fan of this little plant!"

# NIGHTSHADE FAMILY (Solanaceae)

There are 75 genera in the Nightshade family and 3,000 species worldwide. Eight genera are found in Washington. Many are toxic, and many are good foods.

The nightshade plant, showing leaf shape, flowers, and immature fruits

## BLACK NIGHTSHADE
### *Solanum nigrum* and *S. americanum*

There are approximately 1,500 species of *Solanum* in the world, with 10 found in Washington. *S. americanum* is a native; *S. nigrum* is introduced. You are more likely to find *S. nigrum* in Washington, and it's difficult to distinguish from *S. americanum*.

**Use:** Fruits eaten when ripe, raw or cooked

**Range:** Disturbed soils, urban areas

**Similarity to toxic species:** According to many, this is a toxic species, meaning don't eat the raw green fruits, and don't eat the leaves raw. Sickness is possible in either case. There is also a slight resemblance to jimsonweed, which is in the same family.

**Best time:** Summer

**Status:** Somewhat common in weedy areas

**Tools needed:** None

## PROPERTIES

The very young plant much resembles lamb's quarter, except that nightshade doesn't have an erect stem. Rather, it's more widely branched. Also, though the individual leaves of both nightshade and lamb's quarter are quite similar, nightshade lacks the mealy coating of lamb's quarter and lacks the often-noticeable red in the axil of the leaf that is common in lamb's quarter.

The five-petaled white to lavender flower is a very typical Nightshade family flower, resembling the flowers of garden tomatoes. The fruits begin as tiny BB-size green fruits, and by August ripen into little purplish-black "tomatoes." We've eaten the listed *Solanum* species with no problems.

## USES

The fruit of this plant seems to peak around August, when the plant can be prolifically in fruit if the season's rain and heat have been just right. Regardless, I have found ripe fruit of the black nightshade during every month.

You don't want to eat these fruits raw while they are still green, as this could result in a stomachache and minor sickness. They should first be boiled, fried, or otherwise cooked. I will, on the other hand, try a few of the dark purple ripe fruits if I see them while hiking. I like the fresh tartness. It's very much like eating a tomato, but a bit spicier. They are great added to salads—just like adding tomatoes!

But just like tomatoes, there are many other ways to enjoy the ripe black nightshade fruit. We've smashed them and added them to pizza dough. They taste like potatoes, but turn nearly black when cooked. They are good added to soup too. You don't need to cut or slice them, since they are so small. Just toss them into your soup or stew.

Also, just like sun-dried tomatoes with their unique flavor, you can let black nightshade berries dry in the sun (or in your oven or food dryer) and then eat as

The leaves and fruits of nightshade HELEN WONG

The dark purple fruits are ripe.

is or reconstitute later into various recipes. Though it isn't absolutely necessary, I find that they dry quicker if you gently smash them first—such as on the cookie sheet you'll be drying them on.

## CAUTIONS

While there are other ripe nightshade fruits that could be eaten, we don't advise that you eat any but the ones listed above. Also, do not eat the green berries. Only eat the fully ripe, dark purple berries. Otherwise, sickness could result. Green berries should only be consumed if boiled, fried, or otherwise cooked. Anyone with a tomato sensitivity, or sensitivity to other members of this family (e.g., eggplant, chilies, peppers), should not consume these fruits.

The five-petaled flowers and immature fruit of nightshade

# NETTLE FAMILY (Urticaceae)

The Nettle family includes 50 genera and 700 species worldwide. Two of those genera are found Washington.

Outdoor educator Julia Han examining the stinging nettle plant

A patch of stinging nettle

## STINGING NETTLE
*Urtica dioica* and *U. urens*

Of the forty-five species of *Urtica* worldwide, only two (not counting varieties) are found in Washington.

**Use:** Leaves used for food and for tea; stalks made into fiber

**Range:** Riparian, urban fields, edges of farms, disturbed soils, etc.

**Similarity to toxic species:** While nettle itself is regarded as a mechanical toxin by some botanists, it is safe to eat the cooked greens.

**Best time:** Collect the greens in the spring.

**Status:** Common

**Tools needed:** Gloves, snippers

Outdoor educator Gary Gonzales next to the native creek nettle

Stinging nettle

## PROPERTIES

This perennial generally sends up a single stalk in the winter or spring that can reach about 5 feet tall if undisturbed. The leaves are oblong, with toothed margins, and taper to a point. Both the leaves and the stalks are covered with bristles that cause a stinging irritation when you brush against them.

Though it's a European native, you can find it all over Washington, along streams in the wilderness and in fields and backyards.

## USES

This is one of the plants that kept people fed in Europe during World War II when food was scarce. The nettle plant is common, widespread, and very nutritious.

The young, tender leaf tips of nettle are the best to use, though you could also collect just the leaves later in the season (the stems get too tough). These tender tops can be steamed and boiled, which removes the sting of the nettles. They are tasty as a spinach-like dish, alone or served with butter or cheese or other topping. Also try the water from the boiling—it's delicious!

We've also made delicious stews and soups, which began by boiling the nettle tops. Then we quickly added diced potatoes, some red onions, and other greens.

Young stinging nettle tips that have been rinsed. They will be diced and added to a potato-based soup.

Adrian Gaytan collects wild stinging nettle from his farm, bundles it, and sells the bundles at farmers' markets. It is often sold under the Spanish name *hortiga*.

You can also add some miso powder. Cook until tender and then serve, perhaps with Bragg's Liquid Amino Acid added for some great flavor and nutrition.

This is a vitamin-rich plant, so you'll be getting your medicine when you eat it.

## CAUTIONS

As you will probably learn from personal experience, you get "stung" when you brush up against nettle. This is due to the formic acid within each "needle," which causes a skin irritation. So be careful when you gather nettle greens by wearing gloves or other protection. If you do get the nettle rash, you can treat it with fresh aloe vera gel or the freshly crushed leaves of plants such as chickweed or curly dock.

FORAGER NOTE: Nettles are an undervalued medicine, and herbalists speak highly of the many uses for nettle tea. I have found that drinking nettle tea in the spring helps alleviate the symptoms of pollen allergies.

## RECIPE

### Pascal's Stinging Nettle Hot Sauce

I created this hot sauce through experimentation and really enjoyed it. It has a mild "wild" flavor and was really liked by those who tasted it. It's extremely simple to make. This is a basic recipe, but you can add some of your favorite flavors and ingredients, such as Italian herb, bay leaves, etc. As for supplies, you'll need latex gloves, a blender (or go primitive with a knife and a *molcajete*), jars or bottles, and a metal pot.

5 ounces jalapeño peppers, stemmed and chopped with seeds (not too hot, though)
1 ounce serrano peppers
5 ounces fresh nettle leaves (or young nettles)
Juice from 2 limes
6 garlic cloves
3½ cups apple cider vinegar
1 teaspoon kosher or pickling salt
1 cup water or white wine (I used white wine in my original recipe.)

Blend all the ingredients until smooth. Strain for a thinner sauce, or keep as is for a thicker sauce. Transfer to jars and cover. Refrigerate at least 2 weeks, then enjoy!

—RECIPE FROM PASCAL BAUDAR

# VIOLET FAMILY (Violaceae)

There are 23 genera of this family and about 830 species, around 500 of which are *Viola*, the only genera found in Washington.

Violets (*Viola adunca*) in the wild JEAN PAWEK

## VIOLET
*Viola* spp.
There are at least twenty-five species of *Viola* in Washington, not including varieties.

**Use:** Edible leaves and flowers
**Range:** Widespread, growing in most environments in Washington. You can find them in the prairies, foothills, urban areas, subalpine zones, etc.
**Similarity to toxic species:** None
**Best time:** Spring
**Status:** Common
**Tools needed:** Just a bag for collecting

### PROPERTIES
These are commonly planted as garden plants, and they are hardy. They will spread by their roots and appear to naturalize in areas where they were once

cultivated. In fact, they are very easy to cultivate if you want some nearby for your meals.

Though there is great variety in size and minor leaf characteristics, they all have heart-shaped leaves, usually on a long stem of a few inches. The flowers are white, purple, blue, and even yellow, though the cultivated ones are purple or blue.

Wild *Viola odorata* JEAN PAWEK

## USES

When I learned that you can eat violets, I began collecting the heart-shaped leaves from neighbors' yards as I walked home from school. As I came to recognize them, I noticed that they were very common on the edges of people's yards, probably just going wild from an original planting. I'd pick a few leaves here and a few there, and when I got home, I'd cook them up with a little water and season them with just butter. I loved them!

Note the hardiness of the violet plant. Here it is growing through a driveway crack.

I have collected the tender leaves of spring, washed them and diced them, and added them to omelets. I've even tried some diced and added to ramen soup. They are very versatile, not strongly flavored, and can be added to many dishes.

The leaves are also edible raw, and they add their mild flavor to salads. Some people find the leaves a bit strong or tough in salads, but it's really a matter of personal preference.

The flowers are often used to make jellies, or added to jellies, as well as used in various dessert items. I have had a gelatin product that someone else made using the purple flowers and thought it was very tasty.

# Monocots

These have one cotyledon. Leaf veins are generally parallel from the base or mid-rib, and flower parts are generally in threes.

# WATER PLANTAIN FAMILY (Alismataceae)

There are twelve genera worldwide of this family, with three genera found in Washington. The *Alisma* genus, not treated here, is also an edible genus.

The wapato flower LOUIS-M. LANDRY

## WAPATO
### Sagittaria latifolia

Of the twenty or so species of *Sagittaria*, about six have been spotted in Washington. They are all easily recognized by their arrowhead leaves, always growing in water.

**Use:** Bulbs are used, raw or cooked, but mostly cooked.
**Range:** Considered a North American native, these have been found throughout Washington in the lower wetland elevations, along slow streams, at the edges of marshes and lakes.
**Similarity to toxic species:** Some ornamental plants bear a similarity to this arrowhead leaf.
**Best time:** Collect the tubers in the fall.
**Status:** Somewhat common
**Tools needed:** Possibly waders, or a canoe

## PROPERTIES

This is a fairly easy plant to recognize with its unmistakable arrowhead-shaped leaves, always growing in swampy water or on the edges of lakes or slow streams. The little white three-petaled flowers are typically formed in whorls of three near the top of the naked stalk. The tubers are usually about the size of an egg, white colored. From the base of the leaves forms a network of fine fibrous roots. The tubers will develop at various distances from the base of the leaves, usually a few feet away. The tubers are white with a smooth texture.

## USES

The best time to harvest the tubers is late summer to fall, when the tubers are largest. Once you have located a patch early in the year, you can go back later and collect where you see the dried wapato stalks. There seems to be no easy way to harvest these other than wading into the mud and separating the tubers from the fine roots with your feet.

The wapato's distinctive arrow-shaped leaf LOUIS-M. LANDRY

I have tried simply pulling up the whole plant, and sometimes this works too. But usually I was only able to collect these by wading into the muddy water, loosening the tubers from the roots with my feet and toes, and then collecting them by hand.

Some Indian peoples were known to have collected the wapato tubers by going into the wet areas in a canoe and pulling the plants up from the canoe.

Collect the bigger tubers and leave the rest. The tubers can average about 1 inch in diameter, and can be as small as a marble.

Once they are washed, you would use them in any of the ways you might use potatoes: boiled, fried, and baked. They are tasty, though the similarity to actual potatoes is slight. Though these can be eaten raw, they sometimes impart an irritation to the throat. To be safe, if you want to use as a salad food, boil first, chill, and then add other salad ingredients like tomatoes, hard-boiled eggs, dressing, etc.

This tuber was once an important staple for Northwestern native peoples, including the Chinookan of the lower Columbia River, who gave the plant this name.

Wapato tubers KYLE CHAMBERLAIN

# ONION (OR GARLIC) FAMILY (Alliaceae)

There are 13 genera and 750–800 species of the Onion family worldwide. (Some texts still refer to this group as part of Amaryllidaceae.)

The flowers of *Allium bisceptrum* JEAN PAWEK

## WILD ONIONS and others
### *Allium* spp.

There are about 750–800 species of *Allium* worldwide, with about twenty-two in Washington. Most are natives. Some common ones include *Allium acuminatum*, *A. cernuum* (nodding onion), *A. douglasii*, *A. schoenoprasum*, *A. validum*, and *A. vineale*.

**Use:** Bulbs and greens eaten raw or cooked. However, I strongly advise the reader to leave the bulbs in the ground and only pick the greens for food.

**Range:** Can be found in just about every type of environment in Washington

**Similarity to toxic species:** See "Cautions."

**Best time:** The leaves and flowers are most noticeable in the spring and early summer.

**Status:** Though you will not find wild onions in certain areas, they can be common locally.

**Tools needed:** None

Note the size of the root of this wild onion. We advocate eating only the leaves and letting the bulbs remain in the ground.

A native wild onion growing in a pot at a native plant nursery. Though there is great variation among wild onions, they will typically seem like small "green onions."

## PROPERTIES

Wild onions go by many names: ramps, wild garlic, leeks, etc. In general, they look like small "green onions" from the market, though many are inconspicuous when not in flower.

There is a small underground bulb, and the leaves are green and hollow. The flower stalk tends to be a bit more fibrous than the leaves. There appear to be six petals of the same color, but in fact there are three sepals underneath the three identical petals, giving the appearance of a six-petaled flower. The expedient field key to identifying a wild onion is the unmistakable aroma. If you don't have that aroma, you shouldn't use the plant; similar-appearing members of the Lily family could be toxic or poisonous.

Wild onions can be found all over the United States in a broad diversity of eco-types. In Washington we find a lot in the eastern regions and in higher-elevation meadows and fields. We notice them mostly when they flower, because otherwise they appear very much like grass.

## USES

When you find wild onions, you'll be tempted to pull up the plant so you can eat the bulb. That's what you probably do in your own garden, but that's not the only way you can use these. Generally, I only pick the green leaves for consumption. If there are a lot of them, I might take some of the bulbs to eat, then break up the cluster and replant some. The reason I generally only eat the greens is that I've seen some patches of wild onions disappear entirely due to foragers uprooting the whole plant.

So while the wild onion bulbs can be used in any of the myriad ways in which you're used to eating garlic, onions, chives, leeks, and the like, you'll still get most of the flavor and most of the nutritional benefits by eating only the leaves. I pinch off a few leaves here, a few there, and add them to salads. Diced, they're great in soups, stews, egg dishes, and stir-fries. And if you ever have to live off MREs, you can spice them up—and add to their nutritional value—by adding wild onion greens.

All tender parts of wild onions are edible, above- and belowground. Generally, the older flower stalks become fibrous and unpalatable. Otherwise, the bulbs and leaves are all used raw or cooked. Simply remove any outer fibrous layers of the plant, rinse, and then use in any of the ways you'd use green onions or chives.

Wild onions can be added to salads, used as the base for a soup, cooked alone as a "spinach," chopped and mixed into eggs, cooked as a side to fish, and used to enhance countless other recipes. Wild onions share many of the healthful benefits of garlic, and improve any urban or wilderness

The Onion family used to be a part of the Lily family, and both have similar floral characteristics. Each flower is composed of three sepals underneath and three petals above. In this family, the sepals and petals appear identical, giving the impression of six petals.

Overall size of the wild onion

The flowers of *Allium hyalinum* JEAN PAWEK

meal. Backpackers who are relying on dried trail rations will certainly enjoy the sustenance of wild onions. Many American Indians heavily relied on wild onions and regarded them as a staple, not just a condiment.

Excellent health benefits are associated with eating any members of this group. Some of these benefits include lowering cholesterol levels, preventing flu, and reducing high blood pressure. Used externally, the crushed green leaves can be applied directly to wounds to prevent infection.

## CAUTIONS
Never forget that some members of the Lily family with bulbs can be poisonous if eaten. Wild onions used to be classified in the Lily family because their characteristics are so similar. Make absolutely certain that you have correctly identified any wild onions you intend to eat. You should check the floral characteristics to be certain that there are three sepals and three petals. Then you must detect an obvious onion aroma. If there is no onion aroma, do not eat the plant. Though there are a few true onions that lack the onion aroma, it is imperative that you have absolutely identified those nonaromatic species as safe before you prepare them for food.

# ASPARAGUS FAMILY (Asparagaceae)

There are three genera in this relatively new family, created out of the Lily family (Liliaceae). Asparagaceae contains about 320 species, the majority of which (about 300) are a part of the *Asparagus* genus. There are twelve genera of this family in Washington.

Wild asparagus shoots are identical to farm-grown, though typically a bit smaller.

## WILD ASPARAGUS

*Asparagus officinalis*

Of the approximately 300 species of *Asparagus*, this is the only one recorded in Washington.

**Use:** Young shoots eaten

**Range:** Not common west of the Cascades; more common in eastern Washington

**Similarity to toxic species:** See "Cautions."

**Best time:** Spring

**Status:** Common in areas

**Tools needed:** Knife, bag

## PROPERTIES

The edible part of this European native are the first spring shoots, which are identical to the cultivated plant. Have you ever seen an asparagus spear in the produce store or at a farmers' market? Now you know what wild asparagus looks like! Wild asparagus can be an escapee from gardens and farms, and would not be uncommon along a road or trail.

As the asparagus shoot continues to grow, numerous stems grow out of the main shoot. As these stems and their ferny leaves mature, the overall appearance of the plant begins to resemble a 3- to 5-foot-tall ferny bush. As the shoots grow, they become intricately branched, giving the

The asparagus plant grows up into a "ferny" plant, with red fruits as it matures. JIM ROBERTSON

entire plant a ferny appearance. Eventually the plant develops ¼-inch-long, bell-like green flowers that are followed by small berries, dark green at first, then maturing to red.

## USES

Wild and cultivated asparagus are more or less identical. The wild shoots can be used in all the ways in which you'd use store-bought asparagus. They can be steamed or boiled and served with butter, cheese, whatever. They can be made into soup or added to soups and stews, even eaten raw in salads.

The plant is inedible once it has grown to the point of being highly branched.

## CAUTIONS

Eating raw asparagus shoots and the small red berries causes a mild dermatitis reaction in some individuals. Do not eat the red berries of the maturing plant. Consume only the newly emerging shoots.

Wild asparagus plant in fruit DR. AMADEJ TRNKOCZY

Blue flowers of the edible camas ZOYA AKULOVA

## CAMAS
*Camassia quamash* and *C. leichtlinii*

There are just the two species of *Camassia* in Washington, though botanists have defined four subspecies of *C. quamash*. (Outside of Washington, there are at least four other species of *Camassia*, all of which are edible—formerly classified in the Lily family, Liliaceae, and sometimes classified in the Century Plant family, Agavaceae.)

**Use:** The bulbs are the traditional food of this plant.

**Range:** Though once widespread, urban development has wiped out many of the traditional sites. Found in wet and well-drained soils on both sides of the Cascades. Most common in the Columbia Basin. Tends to grow in wet soils, rarely in dry soils.

**Similarity to toxic species:** Death camas. See notes under "Cautions."

**Best time:** Gather the bulbs in late spring to early summer.

**Status:** Certainly less common than in the past; making a comeback as a garden plant

**Tools needed:** A trowel or shovel

## PROPERTIES

Traditionally a part of the Lily family, this perennial lily-like plant consists of a deep bulb from which grasslike leaves arise. The leaves are all basal, flat, up to 1 inch wide and anywhere from 5 to 15 inches in length. The flower stalks may be up to 2 feet tall. The purple flowers are over 1 inch wide, consisting of three sepals and three petals that both look alike, so it appears to have six purple petals. There are six stamens and a three-part pistil.

As the flower matures, the fruit enlarges, which is a three-lobed dry capsule about 1 inch long, full of the black seeds.

Though most commonly found in the Columbia Basin, the camas can be found as far east as Wyoming, and from the Canadian border south into California.

The edible camas plant with its blue flowers JEAN PAWEK

## USES

Camas bulbs—up to 1 inch in diameter—were once one of the most important foods for indigenous peoples. There are still places where you can find them abundantly. When you find them and want to eat them, dig the largest and rebury the smaller ones. To be safe, especially if you are just beginning, only dig the bulbs of those plants that are in flower.

You don't eat these raw—they will cause upset stomach and severe flatulence. They need to be baked for about a day, or more. Traditionally, these were baked from one to three days in a fire pit. A hole is dug, lined with rocks, and a fire is built and burned

The edible camas bulb KYLE CHAMBERLAIN

for at least three hours. Layers of grass and edible vegetation are laid down, and then a layer of clean cotton can be laid down to keep the bulbs clean. The bulbs are then covered with a layer of more edible vegetation and covered with soil. You can dig these out in twelve hours or so, but up to three days is better.

John Kallas (Wild Food Adventures) found that by cooking the bulbs for nine hours in a pressure cooker at 257°F, he produced a sweet-tasting bulb. If you don't have a pressure cooker, you can simply try stovetop cooking, though it takes about twenty-four hours to make the bulbs digestible and tasty. The longer the better—just don't let your pan go dry.

The bulbs can be eaten once processed, and can be dried and powdered and then used in making breads, biscuits, gravy, etc.

In sum, don't eat these raw—and make absolutely certain you have the right bulb.

## LEWIS AND CLARK

The journals have more information about this plant than any other plant they encountered. On September 20, 1805, Clark described how they were searching for food and came upon an Indian village where they were given buffalo meat, dried berries and salmon, and some round roots. He described the roots as "much like an onion, which they call quamash the Bread or Cake is called Pas-she-co Sweet, of this they make bread & Supe they also gave us the bread made of this root all of which we eate heartily."

Clark went on to explain how the camas bulbs were cooked in a traditional fire pit, but didn't say how long they were cooked. He wrote, "I find myself verry unwell all the evening from eateing the fish & roots too freely." Other members of the party also had intestinal pains, which lasted for days. The camas roots were probably not cooked long enough.

Once steamed in the pits, Lewis wrote on June 11, 1806, how the camas bulbs were further processed by the Indians. He noted that the roots were dried in

Mature camas seed ROGER GEORGE

the sun, where they become black and "of a sweet and agreeable flavor." He added, "If the design is to make bread or cakes of the roots they undergo a second process . . . reduced to the consistency of dough and then rolled [into] cakes of eight or ten lbs are returned to the sweat." Once the dough is removed from the fire pit the second time, they are made into little cakes about ½ to ¾ inch thick and dried in the sun or by the fire. According to Lewis, these cakes "will keep sound for a great length of time. This bread or the dried roots are frequently eaten alone by the natives with further preparation, and when they have them in abundance they form an ingredient in almost every dish they prepare. This root is palateable but disagrees with me in every shape I have used it."

Camas flowers and maturing seed capsules, photographed outside Seattle JAY HARTMAN

## CAUTIONS

## DEATH CAMAS
### Zigadenus elegans

A plant known as death camas closely resembles the edible camas. Death camas typically grows in drier soils, and its flower is greenish white, sometimes described as yellow. However, the territories of both can overlap.

It's easy to tell these plants apart when they are in flower, but there are reports of indigenous peoples getting very sick when death camas bulbs were accidentally dug up and included with edible bulbs. (Death is apparently somewhat rare if you eat the death camas, but you'll get seriously ill.)

The overall plant—leaves and bulbs—of the death camas is very similar to the edible camas, though the flowers are smaller and greenish white. In fact, there are at least twenty species of the death camas, mostly in the *Zigadenus* genus, though botanists have been doing a lot of reclassifying of these species.

Bottom line: The edible camas has the blue flower, which can fade to a pale color, somewhat resembling the death camas. So if you're uncertain, don't eat it! Death camas will never have the bright blue flower of the edible camas, so if you only collect when the plant is in flower, you'll be okay.

The toxic death camas plant. Make sure you know how to distinguish the edible blue camas from the death camas. JEAN PAWEK

Greenish-white flowers of the death camas JEAN PAWEK

# RUSH FAMILY (Juncaceae)

The Rush family has 7 genera and 440 species worldwide. In Washington, it is represented by only two genera.

The long *Juncus* shoots, with some of the seeding tops DUDE MCLEAN

## RUSH
### *Juncus textilis* and others

There are 315 species of *Juncus* worldwide. In Washington, forty-nine species (not counting varieties) have been recorded.

**Use:** Tender white growth at base of shoots edible raw or cooked; seeds cooked in pastry or porridge

**Range:** Riparian and coastal areas

**Similarity to toxic species:** In the young stages, there is a superficial resemblance to members of the Lily family, some of which are toxic.

**Best time:** Spring for the shoots; fall for the seeds

**Status:** Common locally

**Tools needed:** None

## PROPERTIES

When seeing *Juncus* for the first time, many folks think it's a type of grass or cattail, or they might say "reed." Yes, it has a grasslike appearance, but there are some important differences that put this plant into a different family.

The leaves are long, grasslike, and hollow from top to bottom. There are various lengths of *Juncus*, and *J. textilis* can be found in thick patches up to 5 to 6 feet tall. The leaves are round in the cross section. The flowers are inconspicuous, bits of seed on the end of long stems, tassel-like, and are formed near the top of each leaf, generally off to one side.

Like many grasses and the cattails, these spread with an underground system of rhizomes. They are typically found in association with wet areas, such as a spring or river, though they are not necessarily right in the water, such as you'd find with watercress.

*Juncus* shoots

## USES

Though this plant and its close relatives are thought of as great weaving and fiber plants, they provide at least two good food sources as well.

Young white base of the *Juncus* shoots

Base of the *Juncus* shoots

In the fall there will be a small tassel of seeds on the top portion of the rushes. If you're there at the right time, you can put a bag under the tassel and shake out the seeds. These seeds are then used in the two ways in which most grains can be used: mixed in with pastry products or cooked as a cereal.

In the spring, when you can gently pull up the long leaves, you will notice that the bottom of the plant is white and tender. There's not a lot of food here, but it's good, and you can get a decent amount in a short period of time. You can eat them raw on the spot or save them to add to salads, stir-fries, or soups.

Harvesting the shoots seems to make the rush patches grow better, but you still shouldn't just pick these for the tender base and then

Daniella Del Valle learns how to weave a basket from the long leaves of the *Juncus* plant.

discard the rest, because you really only get a nibble from each shoot. The upper part of the plant—the long leaves—are great for making traditional baskets. So if you're going to eat some of the young bases, you should really collect the shoots and use them for weaving, or give them to someone who makes baskets. Unless, of course, you're lost and starving, which is a wholly different situation.

# LILY FAMILY (Liliaceae)

The Lily family used to be one of the largest plant families, with nearly 5,000 species included. However, as botanists sought to refine this family, many species were moved to other families, or newly created families, such as the Agave family, Amaryllis family, Asparagus family, Onion family, and others.

Today, botanists include 16 genera, consisting of about 635 species, in this family (Hickman, 2012).

Members of this family are usually perennials, arising from an underground bulb or scaly rhizome. The leaves are lanceolate or grasslike. Flowers, often showy, can be in a raceme or panicle, more or less umbel-like. The flower consists of six perianth segments consisting of three sepals and three petals, which appear identical. There are three or six stamens.

In Washington there are members of eight genera of the Lily family, with at least twenty-eight species.

Flowers of the avalanche lily H. TIM GLADWIN

## AVALANCHE LILY, aka GLACIER LILY, aka DOGTOOTH VIOLET
### *Erythronium grandiflorum*

There are about twenty-five recorded species of the *Erythronium* genus, found mostly in North America, with at least five species identified in Washington.

Avalanche lilies in the field H. TIM GLADWIN

**Uses:** Leaves, flowers, and especially the corms can be eaten.
**Range:** Widespread. Can be found from Alberta to California. Prefers cool and moist mountain meadows.
**Similarity to toxic species:** See "Cautions."
**Best time:** Spring
**Status:** Somewhat common in its environment
**Tools needed:** Digging tool

## PROPERTIES
Sometimes found in dense patches, blooming right after snowmelt. Perennial, up to 1 foot tall, with a single pair of opposite leaves near the base. Leaves are about 1 inch wide and up to 8 inches long. Flowers are yellow to white, with one to four on a single stem. Each flower faces downward. The three sepals and three petals all look alike, so there is the appearance of six yellow petals.

## USES
If these are not abundant, it would be best to just leave them alone and enjoy their beauty. Since all of the plant can be eaten, at least do not dig the corms when there are just a few. You can pick some leaves, even the flowers, and add them to salads or cooked dishes.

Most think of the root as the main food; these are typically found about ½ foot underground, so a digging tool will be needed. The flavor is crisp and good, even sweet. You can enjoy them as a nibble, added to salads, or cooked in any way that you'd cook and blend potatoes.

## CAUTIONS
The avalanche lily is easy to recognize when it's in flower. However, there are many more bulbs from the Lily family than we have listed here, and some can get you sick, even kill you. If you dig a bulb from a plant you've not carefully identified, do not assume it is edible. Never eat the bulb of any plant until you have positively identified it as an edible bulb, and this can usually only be done when you see the plant in flower.

## LEWIS AND CLARK
On a specimen collected southeast of Peck, Idaho, Frederick Posh recorded the following on the expedition's specimen of glacier lily: "From the plains of Columbia near Kooskooskee [today known as Clearwater] R. May 8th 1806. the natives reckon this root as unfitt for food."

# GRASS FAMILY (Poaceae)

There are 650–900 genera worldwide, with about 10,550 species. A massive group! There are so many species that the family is divided into five or six major categories, depending on the botanist. (Some botanists are joiners, some are splitters; the splitters seem to be getting the upper hand.) In Washington there are over eighty genera and hundreds of species.

The Grass family has the "greatest economic importance of any family," according to botanist Mary Barkworth, citing wheat, rice, maize, millet, sorghum, sugarcane, forage crops, weeds, and thatching, weaving, and building materials.

Wild oats

**Use:** Leaves for food (sprouts, juiced, etc.); seeds for flour or meal; some are obviously better than others.

**Range:** Grasses are truly found "everywhere."

**Similarity to toxic species:** See "Cautions."

**Best time:** Somewhat varies depending on what grass we're talking about, but generally spring for the greens and summer to fall for seed.

**Status:** Very common

**Tools needed:** None

## PROPERTIES

The large plant family Poaceae (formerly Gramineae) is characterized by mostly herbaceous but sometimes woody plants with hollow and jointed stems, narrow sheathing leaves, petalless flowers borne in spikelets, and fruit in the form of seedlike grain. It includes bamboo, sugarcane, numerous grasses, and cereal grains such as barley, corn, oats, rice, rye, and wheat.

Grasses are generally herbaceous. They can range from little annuals to giant bamboos. The stems are generally round and hollow, with swollen nodes. The leaves are alternate, generally narrow linear sheathing leaves, with petalless flowers formed in spikelets and fruit in the form of seedlike grain. The flowering and seed structures are rather diverse, ranging from the sticky seeds of the foxtail grasses that get caught in your socks, to the open clusters of sorghum, to such seeds as rice

One of the many grasses found throughout the state

and wheat and the cobs of corn. Indeed, whole books have been written describing the diversity of this large family.

## USES

The edibility of the wild grasses, generically, can be summed up in two categories: the young leaves and the seeds.

You may have had some of the leaf when you went to a health food store and ordered "wheatgrass juice." That's perhaps one of the best ways to eat various grass leaves—juice them. You can purchase an electric juicer or a hand-crank juicer. I have juiced various wild grass leaves and found the flavor to be quite diverse. Some have the flavor of wheatgrass juice and are good added to drinks

Collecting wild grass seeds

or soup broth. Some are very different, almost like seaweed, and these are typically better in soup.

However you do it, get the grasses as young as possible. They are most nutritious at this stage and are less fibrous. You will discover that grasses contain *a lot* of fiber once you start to crank a hand juicer and watch as the green liquid gold comes out one end and the strands of fiber come out the other end. If you don't have a juicer, you could eat the very young grass leaves in salads or cooked soups, though you may find yourself chewing and chewing and spitting out fiber.

The seeds of all grasses are theoretically edible, though harvesting them is very difficult—if not next to impossible—in some cases. Some grass seeds are easy to collect by hand. They are then winnowed. Some are very easy to winnow of the outer chaff; some are more problematic. I have put "foxtail" grass seeds in a small metal strainer and passed them through a fire in order to burn off the outer

Winnowing the chaff from grass seed using the light wind, pouring from one hand to the other

covering. Though I was left with a little seed, I found this method less fruitful than simply locating other grasses with more readily harvestable seeds.

In Washington you might do best to learn a few common useful grasses at first, like Indian rice grass and fowl manna grass.

The seeds you gather for food should be mature and have no foreign growths on them. Then you either grind them into flour for pastry products (bread, biscuits, etc.) or cook into a cereal-like mush.

With thousands of species worldwide on every landmass, and large numbers found in Washington, grasses are a group that we should get to know better. Not only are they arguably more important than trees in holding the earth together—their combined root systems are vast—but they are a valuable food source, assuming you are there at the right time to harvest the seed or leaf.

## CAUTIONS

Be aware that many substances are added to lawns and golf courses to keep the grasses green and bug-free. Those grasses *could* get you sick, so harvest with caution and common sense. Also, make sure that any seed you harvest is mature and free from any mold. Mold will typically give the grain a color, such as green, white, or black. Do not eat moldy grass seeds.

# CATTAIL FAMILY (Typhaceae)

The Cattail family contains two genera and about thirty-two species worldwide.

Angelo Cervera with freshly gathered green cattail spikes. These will be boiled, buttered, and eaten like corn on the cob.

## CATTAIL

*Typha* spp.

The *Typha* genus contains about fifteen species worldwide, with at least four of those species in Washington, including *T. latifolia* and *T. angustifolia*.

**Use:** Food (inner rhizome, young white shoots, green female spike, yellow male pollen); leaves excellent for fiber craft where high tensile strength is not required

**Range:** Wetlands

**Similarity to toxic species:** None

**Best time:** Generally, the shoots and spikes are best collected in the spring. The rhizome could be collected at any time.

**Status:** Common in wetlands

**Tools needed:** Clippers, possibly a trowel

### PROPERTIES

Cattail was one of the plants that helped people survive in Europe during World War II when food was scarce. Everyone everywhere knows cattail—think of it as that grassy plant in the swamps that looks like a hot dog on a stick. Always growing in slow-moving waters or the edges of streams, there are the long flat leaves

The green cattail spike of spring RICK ADAMS.

The cattail spike matures to a brown color, and is no longer edible.

that grow up to 6 feet and taller. These long leaves arise from the underground horizontal rhizomes. When the plants flower in spring, the flower spike is green, with yellowish pollen at the top. As it matures, the green spike ripens to a brown color, creating the familiar fall decoration.

## USES

Euell Gibbons used to refer to cattails as the "supermarket of the swamps," which is a good description of this versatile plant. There are at least four good food sources from the cattail, which I'll list in order of my preference.

In the spring, the plant sends up its green shoots. If you get to them before they get stiff and before the flower spike has started, you can tug them up; the shoot breaks off from the rhizome. You then cut the lower foot or so and peel off the green layers. The inner white layer is eaten raw or cooked. It looks like a green onion, but the flavor is like cucumber.

The spike is the lower part of the flower spike, technically the female part of the flower. You find the spike in spring, when it's entirely green and tender.

Young shoots of the cattail before they have flowered and become fibrous. The lower white section can be eaten raw in salads or cooked with other vegetables.

Though you could eat it raw, it's far better boiled. Cook it like corn on the cob, butter it, and eat it like corn on the cob. Guess what? It even tastes like corn on the cob. You could also scrape off the green edible portion from the woody core and add to stews or stir-fries, or even shape into patties (with egg or flour added) and cook like burgers.

The pollen is the fine yellow material that you can shake out of the flower spikes. The flower spike is divided into two sections: the lower female part, which can be eaten like corn on the cob, and, directly on top, the less-substantial male section, which produced the fine yellow pollen. If you're in the swamp at the right time, typically April or May, you can shake lots of pollen into a bag, then strain it (to remove twigs and bugs), and use it in any pastry product.

The rhizome is also a good starchy food. You get into the mud and pull out the long horizontal roots. Wash them, and then peel off the soft outer layer. You could just chew on the inner part of the rhizome if you need the energy from the natural sugar, or you could process it a bit. One method of processing involves mashing or grinding up the inner rhizome and then putting it in a jar of water. As the water settles, the pure starch will be on the bottom and the fiber will be

The mature cattail spike is now breaking open, revealing the cottony "fluff," which helps scatter the seeds. This downy material can be used as a fire starter, to stop bleeding, and for insulation.

floating on the top, so you can easily scoop it out and discard it. The starch is then used in soups or in pastry and bread products.

Aside from cooking, the long green leaves have a long history of being used for various woven products that will not be under tension, such as baskets, sandals, and hats—even for outer layers of the dwellings utilized by many West Coast Native Americans.

And when that cattail spike matures to a chocolate-brown color, it can be broken open to reveal an insulating fluff. Each tiny seed is actually connected to a bit of fluff that aids in the transportation of that seed to greener grass on the other side. You can use that fluff to stop the bleeding of a minor wound, as an alternative to down when stuffing a sleeping bag or coat, and as a fantastic fire starter!

# OTHER EDIBLES

Do you have a favorite Washington wild food that wasn't listed here?

There are many others out there that could make a meal, or part of a meal, especially when conditions are adverse. Yes, prickly pear cactus grows in the sagebrush-steppe area, but it's nothing like the cactus pads you'll find in the Southwest. Washington's prickly pear pads are thinner, and full of glochids and thicker spines. Yes, in an emergency you could peel a prickly pear pad and eat it, but it's not likely to ever be a regular part of your diet, even if you live in the Columbia Plateau.

Chocolate lily (*Fritillaria lanceolata*) is edible but not abundant. Shooting stars are another possibility, as is stonecrop, which is okay as a garnish but not especially common.

And there are many more, especially when you include all the introduced exotic species that can be found in all settlements.

But remember, our intent was to include only those plants that are the most widespread throughout the state and readily recognizable, and those that would make a significant contribution to your day-to-day meals. We also wanted to have plants that represented most of the biological zones in the state. Additionally, we don't want you eating any endangered or rare species, so they've not been included. This book was compiled based on what we ascertained were the plants you are most likely to be eating from the wild, most of the time.

Still, if you feel we've left out an important plant that you have found useful on a regular basis, please write and let us know. If feasible, we'll include that plant in a future edition of this book.

As you continue your study of ethnobotany, you will discover that there are many more wild plants that could be used for food. Some are marginal, and some just aren't that great.

In fact, there are *many* other wild Washington greens, fruits, roots, and nuts that I have eaten, even some I never found described in a wild-food or ethnobotany book. Yes, many are "edible," but after trying them, I realized why ancient peoples never used some of them, or only used them when nothing else was available. That's the real meaning of the term *starvation food*—you'd only eat it if you actually had next to nothing else to eat.

Yes, there are many wild animals and ocean life that could be used for food—fish, snakes, lizards, birds, small mammals, insects, etc.—but this book is about the plants.

## The Study of Mycology

Some of the books in the *Foraging* series have chosen to include a few common mushrooms into the mix of wild plants that you can bring into your kitchen. After much thought, I have chosen not to. If you're interested in adding mushrooms to your wild-food diet, please get a copy of the FalconGuide *Mushrooms of Washington* to use as a companion to this guide.

While there are many readily recognized edible fungi, I never ate wild mushrooms on my own until I'd spent about two years of active study and fieldwork. There are also many, many fungi that are not well known with regard to edibility. Some, of course, are deadly.

If you want to begin using wild mushrooms for food, I am of the opinion that you should plan on spending as much time as you devote to at least a four-unit college course for at least two semesters, preferably more.

There are many reasons for this. For the most part, you cannot go back day after day to the same mushroom to study it in detail and watch its growth cycle. Mushrooms come suddenly and decompose just as rapidly. They are not like the oak tree that will be there every day.

Not all mushrooms have been identified, and even less is known about the edibility of most species. And in their attempt to further clarify the relationships of mushrooms, mycologists occasionally rename a mushroom. The changes in Latin names cause initial confusion to wild-food foragers. And though I regularly eat about two dozen wild mushrooms, I am always humbled by the occasional newspaper article describing how a lifelong mycologist ate the wrong mushroom and died!

There are many books and videos today that are exclusively devoted to giving you an understanding of how mushrooms grow, their classification, and how to accurately identify those that are edible. Even better than books and videos are classes and clubs where you go into the field and see the mushrooms for yourself.

For those of you who are seriously interested in identifying and eating wild mushrooms, I encourage you to enroll in a mycology course at a local college, or join a local mushroom group. There are many such groups nationwide, including several in the state of Washington. (If you cannot find one, contact me and I will try to find one close to you.) You owe it to your longevity to take the time to learn about mushrooms directly with someone who has already done so. You need to learn about the different types of fungi, and why they grow where and when they grow. You need to see these mushrooms in the field, and see how they develop throughout their usually short growing period.

# TEST YOUR KNOWLEDGE OF PLANTS

Here is a simple test that I use in my classes. Take the test for plants, and see how you do.

1. ☐ True. ☐ False. Berries that glisten are poisonous.
2. ☐ True. ☐ False. White berries are all poisonous.
3. ☐ True. ☐ False. All blue and black berries are edible.
4. ☐ True. ☐ False. If uncertain about the edibility of berries, watch to see if the animals eat them. If animals eat the berries, the berries are good for human consumption.
5. Would you follow the following advice? State yes or no, and give reason.

   According to *Food in the Wilderness* authors George Martin and Robert Scott, "If you do not recognize a food as edible, chew a mouthful and keep it in the mouth. If it is very sharp, bitter, or distasteful, do not swallow it. If it tastes good, swallow only a little of the juice. Wait for about eight hours. If you have suffered no nausea, stomach or intestinal pains, repeat the same experiment swallowing a little more of the juice. Again, wait for eight hours. If there are no harmful results, it probably is safe for you to eat. (This test does not apply to mushrooms.)"

6. ☐ True. ☐ False. "A great number of wilderness plants are edible but generally they have very little food value" (Martin and Scott, *Food in the Wilderness*).
7. ☐ True. ☐ False. Bitter plants are poisonous.
8. ☐ True. ☐ False. Plants that exude a milky sap when cut are all poisonous.
9. ☐ True. ☐ False. Plants that cause stinging or irritation on the skin are all unsafe for consumption.

**10.** The illustration to the right is the typical flower formation for all members of the Mustard family. Write out the formula:

_____ petal(s); _____ sepal(s);
_____ stamen(s); _____ pistil(s).

**11.** Of what value is it to be able to identify the Mustard family?

**12.** ❐ True. ❐ False. Mustard (used on hot dogs) is made by grinding up the yellow flowers of the mustard plant.

**13.** ❐ True. ❐ False. Yucca, century plant, and prickly pear are all members of the Cactus family.

**14.** ❐ True. ❐ False. There are no poisonous cacti.

**15.** ❐ True. ❐ False. Plants that resemble parsley, carrots, and fennel are all in the Carrot (or Parsley) family and are thus all safe to eat.

**16.** ❐ True. ❐ False. Only seventeen species of acorns are edible. The rest are toxic.

**17.** To consume acorns, the tannic acid must first be removed. Why?

**18.** If you are eating no meat or dairy products (during a survival situation, for example), how is it possible to get complete protein from plants alone?

**19.** ❐ True. ❐ False. There are no toxic grasses.

**20.** ❐ True. ❐ False. Seaweeds are unsafe survival foods.

**21.** ❐ True. ❐ False. All plants that have the appearance of a green onion and have the typical onion aroma can be safely eaten.

**22.** List all of the plant families (or groups) from this lesson that we've identified as entirely or primarily nontoxic:

## ANSWERS

1. False. Insufficient data.

2. False. Though mostly true, there are exceptions, such as white strawberry, white mulberry, and others. Don't eat any berry unless you know its identity and know it to be edible.

3. False. Mostly true, but there are some exceptions. Don't eat any berry unless you've identified it as an edible berry.

4. False, for several reasons. Certain animals are able to consume plants that would cause sickness or death in a human. Also, animals *do* occasionally die from eating poisonous plants—especially during times of drought. Also, just because you watched the animal eat a plant doesn't mean the animal didn't get sick later!

5. *Very* bad advice, even though this has been repeated endlessly in "survival manuals" and magazine articles. Since food is rarely your top "survival priority," this is potentially dangerous advice.

6. False. To verify that this is not so, look at *Composition of Foods*, which is published by the US Department of Agriculture. In many cases, wild foods are far more nutritious than common domesticated foods.

7. False. Insufficient data. Many bitter plants are rendered edible and palatable simply by cooking or boiling.

8. False. Though you can't eat any of the euphorbias, many others (like dandelion, lettuce, milkweed, sow thistle) exude a milky sap. Forget about such "short-cuts." Get to know the individual plants.

9. False. Many edible plants have stickers or thorns that must first be removed or cooked away, such as nettles, cacti, etc.

10. Mustard flowers are composed of:

    4 sepals (1 under each petal)

    4 petals (the colorful part of the flower)

    1 pistil (in the very center of the flower, the female part of the flower)

    6 stamens, 4 tall and 2 short (The 6 stamens surround the pistil.)

11. There are no poisonous members of the Mustard family.

12. False. The mustard condiment is made by grinding the seeds. Yellow is typically from food coloring.

13. False. Only the prickly pear is a cactus.

14. True, but you must know what is, and is not, a cactus. There are some very bitter narcotic cacti, which you would not eat due to unpalatability. Also, some euphorbias closely resemble cacti and will cause sickness if eaten.

Euphorbias exude a milky sap when cut; cacti do not. Any fleshy, palatable part of true cacti can be eaten.

15. False. The Carrot (or Parsley) family contains both good foods and deadly poisons. Never eat any wild plant resembling parsley unless you have identified that specific plant as an edible species.

16. False. All acorns can be consumed once shelled and leached of their tannic acid.

17. Tannic acid is bitter.

18. Combine the seeds from grasses with the seeds from legumes. This generally produces a complete protein. For details, see *Diet for a Small Planet* by Frances Moore Lappé.

**Traditional Diets that Combine Legumes and Grass Seeds to Make a Complete Protein**
Loosely based on "Summary of Complementary Protein Relationships," Chart X in *Diet for a Small Planet* by Lappé.

|  | Legumes | Grasses |
|---|---|---|
| Asian diet | Soy (miso, tofu, etc.) | Rice |
| Mexican diet | Beans (black beans, etc.) | Corn (tortillas) |
| Middle Eastern diet | Garbanzos | Wheat |
| Southern United States | Black-eyed peas | Grits |
| Starving student | Peanut butter | Wheat bread |
| Others to consider | Mesquite, palo verde, peas, carob, etc. | Millet, rye, oats, various wild grasses, etc. |

19. True. However, be certain that the seeds are mature and have no mold-like growth on them.

20. False. Seaweeds are excellent. Make certain they've not been rotting on the beach, and don't collect near any sewage treatment facilities.

21. True. But be sure you have an onion!

22. All members of the Mustard family, all palatable cacti, all acorns, all cattails, grasses, seaweeds, onions. There are many other "safe" families, but you will need to do a bit of botanical study in order to identify those families. Begin by reading the descriptions of each family in this book. Also study *Botany in a Day* by Tom Elpel.

# THE DOZEN EASIEST-TO-RECOGNIZE, MOST WIDESPREAD, MOST VERSATILE WILD FOODS OF WASHINGTON

In the mid-1970s I began to investigate the edibility of whole plant families and found that there were quite a few entire families that are safe to eat, given a few considerations in each case. Some of these families are difficult to recognize unless you are a trained botanist. Still, in this book I have described many of the entirely safe families. My original research on this was done with Dr. Leonid Enari, who was one of my teachers and the chief botanist at the Los Angeles County Arboretum in Arcadia, California.

The chart below was the idea of my friend Jay Watkins, who long urged me to produce a simple handout on the dozen most-common edible plants that everyone should know. Granted, there are many more than a dozen, but as Jay and I discussed this idea, I decided to focus on twelve plants that could be found not just anywhere in the United States, but in most locales throughout the world. The result was the accompanying chart, which is largely self-explanatory.

This chart assumes that you already know these plants, since its purpose is not identification. Anyone who has studied wild foods for a few years is probably already familiar with all these plants. However, not everyone is aware that these plants are found worldwide.

This overview should help beginners as well as specialists. It is merely a simple comparative chart, which could be expanded to many, many pages. It is deliberately kept short and simple.

|  | Description | Parts Used | Food Uses | Preparation | Benefits | Where Found | When Found |
|---|---|---|---|---|---|---|---|
| **Acorns** | The fruit of the oak tree | Acorns (nuts) | Flour, pickles, mush | Leach out tannic acid first, then grind. | Similar to potatoes | Mountains, valleys | Fall |
| **Cactus** | Succulent desert plants of various shapes | Tender parts; fruit | Salad; cooked vegetable; omelet; dessert; drinks | 1. Carefully remove spines. 2. Dice or slice as needed. | Pads said to be good for diabetics; fruits rich in sugar | Dry desertlike environments; Mediterranean zones | Young green pads in spring and summer; fruit in summer and fall |
| **Cattail** | Reedlike plants; fruit looks like a hot dog on stick | 1. Pollen 2. Green flower spike 3. Tender shoots 4. Rhizome | 1. Flour 2. Cooked vegetable 3. Salads 4. Flour | 1. Shake out pollen. 2. Boil. 3. Remove outer green fibrous parts. 4. Remove outer parts; crush. | Widespread, versatile | Wet areas (e.g., roadside ditches, marshes) | Spring through fall |
| **Chickweed** | Weak-stemmed, opposite leaves, five-petaled flower | Entire tender plant | Salads, tea | Clip, rinse, and add dressing, or make infusion. | Good diuretic | Common and widespread when moisture is present | Spring and summer |
| **Dandelion** | Low plant, toothed leaves, conspicuous yellow flower | 1. Roots 2. Leaves | 1. Cooked vegetable, coffee-like beverage 2. Salads, cooked vegetable | 1. Clean and cook, or dry, roast, grind. 2. Clean and make desired dish. | Richest source of beta-carotene; very high in vitamin A | Common in lawns and fields | Best harvested in spring |
| **Dock** | Long leaves with wavy margins | 1. Leaves 2. Stems 3. Seeds | 1. Salads, cooked vegetable 2. Pie 3. Flour | 1. Clean. 2. Use like rhubarb. 3. Winnow seeds. | Richer in vitamin C than oranges | Common in fields and near water | Spring through fall |

| | Description | Parts Used | Food Uses | Preparation | Benefits | Where Found | When Found |
|---|---|---|---|---|---|---|---|
| **Grasses** | Many widespread varieties | 1. Seeds 2. Leaves | 1. Flour, mush 2. Salads, juiced, cooked vegetable | 1. Harvest and winnow. 2. Harvest, clean, and chop. | 1. Easy to store 2. Rich in many nutrients | Common in all environments | 1. Fall 2. Spring |
| **Lamb's Quarter** | Triangular leaves with toothed margins, mealy surface | 1. Leaves and tender stems 2. Seeds | 1. Salads, soups, omelets, cooked 2. Bread, mush | 1. Harvest and clean. 2. Winnow. | Rich in vitamin A and calcium | Likes disturbed rich soils | Spring through fall |
| **Mustard** | Variable leaves with large terminal lobes; four-petaled flowers | Leaves, seeds, some roots | Salads, cooked dishes, seasoning | Gather, clean, cut as needed. | Said to help prevent cancer | Common in fields and many environments | Spring through fall |
| **Onions** | Grasslike appearance; flowers with three petals, three sepals | Leaves, bulbs | Seasoning, salads, soups, vegetable dishes | Clean and remove tough outer leaves. | Good for reducing high blood pressure and high cholesterol level | Some varieties found in all environments | Spring |
| **Purslane** | Low-growing succulent, paddle-shaped leaves | All tender portions | Salads, sautéed, pickled, soups, vegetable dishes | Rinse off any soil. | Richest source of omega-3 fatty acids | Common in parks, gardens, disturbed soils | Summer |
| **Seaweeds** | Marine algae of many shapes and colors | Entire plant | Depends on seaweed: salads, soups, stews, broth | Use dried, raw, or cooked, depending on species. | Excellent source of iodine; great salt substitute | Oceans | Year-round |

**Latin names:** Acorns = *Quercus* spp.; Cattail = *Typha* spp.; Chickweed = *Stellaria media*; Dandelion = *Taraxacum officinale*; Dock = *Rumex crispus*; Grasses = *Poaceae* (Grass family); Lamb's quarter = *Chenopodium album*; Mustard = *Brassica* spp./Mustard family = Cruciferae; Onions = *Allium* spp.; Purslane = *Portulaca oleracea*; Seaweeds = brown, red, and green marine algae (Phaeophyceae, Rhodophyceae, Chlorophyceae)

# STAFF OF LIFE: BEST WILD-FOOD BREAD SOURCES

Baking of bread goes back to the most ancient cultures on the earth, back when humankind discovered that you could grind up the seeds of grasses, add a few other ingredients, let it rise, and bake it. There are countless variations, of course, but bread was once so nutritious that it was called the "staff of life."

Most likely, the discovery of bread predated agriculture, since the earth was full of wild grasses and a broad assortment of roots and seeds that could be baked into nutritious loaves. Most grains store well for a long time, which allowed people of the time to pursue culture, inner growth, and technology. The development of civilizations and the development of agriculture go hand in hand. And bread was right there from the beginning.

Today we are at another extreme of a very long road of human development. We started with the struggle for survival, and with the surplus of the land allowing us the time to develop more fully in all aspects. That good bread from the earth was heavy, rich, and extremely nutritious. It was a vitamin and mineral tablet.

We produced so much grain that the United States called itself "the bread-basket of the world." And this massive volume resulted in losses in the fields from insects, as well as loss due to spoilage. Thus came the so-called Green Revolution, in which chemical fertilizers replaced time-honored fertilizers such as animal manures, straw and hay, compost, bone meal, and other natural substances that the modern farmer was too busy and too modern to use. Crops increased while the nutritional values dropped. And though this is a gross oversimplification, bread from the supermarket is no longer the staff of life.

The mineral content of the once-rich soils of the United States has steadily declined. Producers process and refine "white flour" and then add certain minerals back in to the bread dough. We sacrificed quality since we thought it would bring us security, and we knew it would bring big bucks. Now, the great irony is that we lost the quality of the food, of the soil, and ultimately we are no more secure than ever before. Why? Because a soil rich in natural organic matter can withstand floods and droughts and the ravages of insects. It is the folly of humans that causes the droughts and plagues of modern times.

There is much—very much—that we need to learn about "modern agriculture" or "agribiz," as it is more appropriately called. We should not put our heads into the sand, ostrich-like, and pretend the problem does not exist.

Personal solutions are many. Grow your own garden. Learn about wild foods, and use them daily. By using common wild plants, you can actually create a nutritious bread comparable to the breads your ancestors ate. The easiest way to get started is to make flour from these wild seeds and mix that flour half-and-half with your conventional flours, such as wheat. You'll end up with a more flavorful, more nutritious bread, pancake, or pastry product.

Once you begin to use your local wild grains, you'll be amazed how tasty, how abundant, and how versatile these wild foods are.

The accompanying chart is by no means complete. It is a general guideline to show you what is available over widespread areas. However, there are quite a few plants of limited range that produce abundant seeds or other parts that are suitable for bread making. In most cases, you should consult any of the many wild-food cookbooks available for details on using each of these wild grains.

Note that "Grass" is a huge category, since it actually includes many of our domestic grains such as wheat, corn, rye, and barley. Though some of the seeds listed in this chart can be eaten raw, most require some processing before you can eat them. Acorns must be soaked or boiled to get rid of the bitter tannic acid. The seed from amaranth, dock, and lamb's quarter can get somewhat bitter and astringent as it gets older and is improved by cooking.

By rediscovering the wealth of wild plants that are found throughout this country, we can bring bread back to its status as the "staff of life."

## RECIPES

### Beginner Wild Bread

1 cup whole wheat flour
1 cup wild flour of your choice
3 teaspoons baking powder
3 tablespoons honey
1 egg
1 cup milk
3 tablespoons vegetable oil
Salt to taste, if desired

Mix all the ingredients well. Bake in oiled bread pans for about 45 minutes at 250°F or in your solar oven until done.

### Beginner Pancake

Follow the above recipe, adding extra milk or water so you have the appropriate pancake batter consistency. Make pancakes as normal.

## "Wild Bread" Chart

| | Part Used | How Processed | Where Found | Palatability | Ability to Store |
|---|---|---|---|---|---|
| Acorns | Shelled acorns | Leach acorns of tannic acid by soaking or boiling; grind into meal. | Worldwide; ripen in fall | Good, if fully leached | Excellent |
| Amaranth | Seeds | Collect and winnow seeds. | Worldwide as a weed of disturbed soils | Good | Very good |
| Cattail | Pollen and rhizome | Shake the top of cattail spikes into bag to collect pollen; mash peeled rhizome and separate out fiber. | Worldwide in wet and marshy areas | Very good | Good |
| Dock | Seeds | Collect brown seeds in fall; rub to remove "wings," and winnow. | Worldwide in wet areas and disturbed soils | Acceptable | Very good |
| Grass—most species | Seeds | Generally, simply collect and winnow; difficulty depends on species. | Worldwide; some found in nearly every environment | Generally very good | Very good to excellent |
| Lamb's Quarter | Seeds | Collect when leaves on plant are dry; rub between hands and winnow. | Worldwide in disturbed soils and farm soils | Acceptable to good | Very good |

**Note:** This chart is intended only as a general guideline to compare sources for "wild bread" ingredients. There may be many other wild plants that can be used for bread. Also, never eat any wild plant that you have not positively identified as an edible species.

**Latin names:** Acorns = *Quercus* spp.; Amaranth = *Amaranthus* spp.; Cattail = *Typha* spp.; Dock = *Rumex crispus*; Grass = Poaceae; Lamb's quarter = *Chenopodium album*

# USEFUL REFERENCES

Angier, Bradford. *Free for the Eating.* Mechanicsburg, PA: Stackpole Books, 1996.

Baldwin, Bruce G., et al., eds. *The Jepson Manual, Vascular Plants of California.* 2nd ed. Berkeley: University of California Press, 2012. This is the book California botanists use, and a vast majority of the plants in California can also be found in Washington.

Benoliel, Doug. *Northwest Foraging: The Classic Guide to Edible Plants of the Northwest.* Seattle: Skipstone Books, 2011. Benoliel covers more than fifty plants in this guide to Northwest edibles, which includes line drawings and a section on poisonous plants. No marginal foods included.

Deur, Douglas. *Pacific Northwest Foraging: 120 Wild and Flavorful Edibles.* Portland, OR: Timber Press, 2014. Beautiful photographs and full of useful information and personal experience.

Elpel, Tom. *Botany in a Day: The Patterns Method of Plant Identification.* Pony, MT: HOPS Press, 2000. Highly recommended. This is the way botany should be taught.

Elpel, Tom, and Kris Reed. *Foraging the Mountain West.* Pony, MT: HOPS Press, 2014. A lively exploration of the wild foods of the Northwest.

Enari, Dr. Leonid. *Plants of the Pacific Northwest.* Portland, OR: Binfords and Mort, 1956. Written by Dr. Enari after he moved to Portland from Estonia, this book covers 663 weeds, wildflowers, shrubs, and trees that are common in the Northwest. Includes 185 line drawings, which means that most plants are not illustrated.

Garcia, Cecelia, and Dr. James Adams. *Healing with Medicinal Plants of the West: Cultural and Scientific Basis for Their Use.* Orinda, CA: Abedus Press, 2005. An excellent summary of the common medicinal plant uses found in the West.

Gibbons, Euell. *Stalking the Blue-Eyed Scallop.* New York: David McKay Company, 1964. A good description of many of the foods found on the Pacific coast.

Hitchcock, C. Leo, and Arthur Cronquist. *Flora of the Pacific Northwest.* Seattle: University of Washington Press, 1981. This is the book the botanists of Oregon and Washington use. As a book of flora goes, it's designed as a key so you can (hopefully) identify the plant you've found. Mostly botanical text; technical line drawings throughout. Also has a good glossary (you'll need it).

Kallas, John. *Edible Weeds: Wild Foods from Dirt to Plate.* Vol. 1 and 2. Salt Lake City, UT: Gibbs Smith, 2010. These two books cover common wild foods, which are some of the most common wild foods not only in Washington but throughout the United States. The full-color volumes tell you everything from identifying the plant to using it in a variety of recipes. Kallas also teaches classes and is the "go-to" guy for the Pacific Northwest when it comes to wild foods! Reach John Kallas, director of Wild Food Adventures at Institute for the Study of Edible Wild Plants and Other Foragables, 4125 N. Colonial Ave., Portland, OR 97217-3338; (503) 775-3828; www.wildfoodadventures.com.

Kirk, Donald. *Wild Edible Plants of Western North America.* Happy Camp, CA: Naturegraph, 1970. Though you generally cannot positively identify plants with this book, it does contain a large number of edible and useful plant descriptions, along with drawings that leave a lot to the imagination. Get this book, and use another book to positively identify the plants.

Moerman, Daniel E. *Native American Ethnobotany.* Portland, OR: Timber Press, 1998. Nearly 1,000 pages of descriptions of how every plant known to be used by Native Americans was utilized. No pictures at all, but an incredible resource all in one book.

Taylor, Ronald J. *Northwest Weeds: The Ugly and Beautiful Villains of Fields, Gardens, and Roadsides.* Missoula, MT: Mountain Press Publishing, 1990. An excellent full-color summary of some of the common plants of the Northwest, organized by families.

"Washington Flora Checklist: A Checklist of the Vascular Plants of Washington State." Hosted by the University of Washington Herbarium. http://biology.burke.washington.edu/herbarium/waflora/checklist.php.

Wayne, Phillips H. *Plants of the Lewis and Clark Expedition.* Missoula, MT: Mount Press Publishing Co., 2003. An excellent botanical journey along the Lewis and Clark Expedition of 1804–1806.

# INDEX

# ABOUT THE AUTHOR

**Christopher Nyerges,** cofounder of the School of Self-Reliance, has led wild-food and survival skills walks for thousands of students since 1974. He has authored sixteen books, mostly on wild foods, survival, and self-reliance, and thousands of newspaper and magazine articles. He continues to teach where he lives in Los Angeles County, California. More information about his classes and seminars is available at www.SchoolofSelf-Reliance.com, or by writing to School of Self-Reliance, Box 41834, Eagle Rock, CA 90041.